The Frogmore Farmer

THE FROGMORE FARMER

BRIAN J. DROMGOLD

Copyright © Brian J Dromgold 2018

All rights reserved. No part of this book may be reproduced or transmitted in any form or by any means, electronic or mechanical, including photocopying, recording or by an information storage and retrieval system, without prior permission in writing from the publisher.

Published by Alexander Publishing

Cover design by Chloe Lester

Typeset by BookPOD

Cataloguing-in-Publication entry is available from the National Library of Australia
http://catalogue.nla.gov.au

ISBN: 978-0-9953567-9-5 (paperback)

FOREWORD

When first asked to write a foreword for this book I went through a gamut of emotions, nervous, what would I say, scared, gosh what if I let them down, then proud, they trust me so I may actually be able to create something.

While reading the book it evoked a lot of memories. First the characters were so well known to me even though they lived in times long gone. The reason they were known to me was from stories regaled to me by my grandmother, mother Pat, Aunties Pauline and Joan as well as Uncle Brian.

While reading this book no actual photographs were present yet in my mind I vividly saw them. Some I actually recall from the family album and others so aptly described they seemed part of my memories. As a matter of fact, I attended the wedding on 31 March 1956 as a two-year-old and many times have seen the photos from the wedding and on the piano. They are crystal clear in my mind.

The people and places so lovingly recalled for a very worthwhile purpose, the purpose of recollection for Brian's children, great grandchildren and beyond. A tale where its longevity will remain in the pages of this book and in Brian's own words perhaps one of the younger family members may take up where he left off and keep his story going.

The story itself is wonderfully written from the heart and honest. It has humour, good times and bad. An honest story of a boy who became a man in adverse times without the 'mod cons' we take for granted and which became a huge part of our daily lives. With no electricity, telephone, indoor toilet or water. The only way to school was to walk or ride a horse. He survived and thrived during this time. His life began in post-depression NSW and followed through the effects of World War II.

This is about a man who is strong, has a great moral compass and has deep love for his family and has instilled these qualities in his own children.

Cheryl Coble
Loving Niece

PREFACE

At the suggestion of my family, I have set down in these pages some recollections from my life.

I've long thought about writing the story of my life. Not because it was extraordinary but because in many ways it's been ordinary. An ordinary story of an Australian bloke. A bloke who grew up poor on a farm, although he didn't always know he was poor. A bloke who left the farm for the big smoke, and grew a family and a life for himself, well away from his roots.

My grandchildren and great-grandchildren have no concept of my early life and I'd like to give them a feel for it. It's a time, like all others, that will never come again, but in so many ways it formed the life they are now leading. Families and genetics are funny things, they do influence who we are. Then there's the circumstances we experience that add to the story. I'm sure the kids now look at an elderly man who has lots of stories—some of which they may not believe, and some of which may seem improbable.

I wish my own ancestors had written about their lives. I'd love to know more about them as people. I suspect I'd be saying, 'Wow, I do that too', or 'That might be why I...'

I hope that one day, just one of my descendants will enjoy this story, identify with parts of it and perhaps learn some things from it, and then add their stories to it, taking up where I leave off. Because that's life and it's a great gift to be able to understand and feel connected to the past and the future.

Brian Dromgold

Many of the aspects of daily life as I was growing up have now gone forever. I was shaped by those times and the people surrounding me during different periods of my life and wanted to share some of those times and experiences.

I promise that all of the recorded events actually happened to me, to the best that my memory recalls.

Brian Dromgold

ACKNOWLEDGEMENTS

Writing this book has been both a trip down memory lane, and an opportunity to reflect on my life.

It's provided an opportunity to talk to old friends, reconnect with family members who have moved away, remember those who've come and gone during my life and ponder the future for those who will go forward.

I thought it would be about the things I've done and experiences I've had; and it is. But more than that it is a reflection and commentary on people. Family, friends, foes and acquaintances. Laughter and tears have been plenty through my life and even more through the writing and reflecting. Diane I guess we can stop buying bulk supplies of tissues now.

I am truly grateful to have had the opportunity to undertake this project and to present the results in this book.

As I said, it's mostly about people and there are those I'd like to mention here for their specific support and contribution. I know I will miss some so please forgive me if you're names not in the list, it doesn't mean I've forgotten you, just the constraints of an aging and tired mind. A mind that is filled with wonder and gratitude for the people in my life.

At the start there were my parents, grandparents and extended country-based family. You've mostly gone on ahead now but there is no doubt of my gratitude for you and the foundation you gave me in life. My Uncle John stands out as the biggest influence and the main contributor to my sense of self and my bravery and determination to pursue the life I wanted rather than the one laid down for me.

Then there are my siblings, three energetic mischievous girls who gave as good as they got and were every bit as enthusiastic for life and adventure as I was. Joan has gone ahead but Pat and Pauline are to this day very close to me and are friends as much as family.

To Del my wife of 62 years – there are no words. We took on the big smoke, took risks, and followed our dreams. Our dreams were modest but as we reflect we wouldn't have wanted anything else. Del you've given me a home and family and love that has endured. It hasn't always been easy, but it's always been worth it.

Our three children, Diane, Christine and Richard. I'm proud of you and impressed that you've each pursued your own dreams and built lives you wanted. That takes courage and bravery. You're each strong independent people with a strong love of family and a determination to do what's right rather than what's easy. Del and I have watched in awe at the choices you've made (and sometimes with trepidation too) and enjoyed the journey with you.

To our grandchildren, Kate, Trevor, Daniel, Tom, Jake, Mathew, Alice and Jennifer. What a treat to have been close to you growing up and watching as you embark of your own dreams and adventures. Don't ever stop doing that. To our great grandchildren (Ned for now and others not yet here) know you come from a long line of strong brave men and women who whether you see them or not are cheering you on. Dream and don't give up – just remember dreams come true after the work is done.

Specifically in relation to bringing this book together I'd like to thank; Diane Dromgold (daughter) who has coordinated everything; Michael Collins and Ian Demack for helping me get it all in the right order with the right words; Helen Wright (Richard's partner), Christine Dromgold, Kate Beinke (granddaughter), Alice Hanks (granddaughter), Amanda Hanks (Alice's wife) and Ian Johnson (Diane's partner) for reading, editing and improving the manuscript; Tom Beinke for coming up with the name for the book; Chloe Lester (Tom's partner) for designing the cover; and Cheryl Coble (niece) for writing the foreword.

Finally, thanks to Sylvie and the team at Alexander publishing who have made a pile of paper into an actual book and through the magic of modern technology made it available in both print and digitally. I can't wait to see a copy on my kindle.

Thanks everyone for your help, love and support. As much as this is my story it's also yours and I hope one day, one of you will write the sequel.

With love,

Brian John Dromgold

CHAPTER ONE

My beginning

My father.

I was born in the Boorowa Hospital on the 26th April 1935. Boorowa, in central NSW, is a farming district known for its wool and its wheat.

My father, Richard Patrick John Dromgold, was 24 years old, while my mother, Elizabeth Greta Dromgold (nee Humphries) was 19. They already had my older sister Patricia at home. Home was a very small cottage on a very remote farm.

There was no electricity, no running water, and no bathroom. They had a fuel stove in the kitchen, two bedrooms and a lounge room. By any measure it was a humble beginning.

I have no memories of those early years, but looking back I can imagine the isolation, loneliness and hardship the family lived through. I never asked Mum but I imagine, after the blush of romance and excitement associated with dating and marrying my father, that she wished she'd taken a different path.

It was a hard life and Dad, like a lot of alcoholics I've known over the years, was not easy to live with. While we never went hungry he wasn't a good provider.

The Dromgolds and the Hortons

On my father's side, the Dromgold family has been traced back to 1791. They were devout Roman Catholics.

Dad's good qualities included being a very hard worker, and having the gift of being able to get on with most people. He didn't enjoy the best start in life. My grandmother had Dad out of wedlock. The man responsible was Richard Platt. He also impregnated another local woman, and subsequently married her, rather than my grandmother.

Bravely, my grandmother kept the baby, which was unusual in those days. Unmarried women who fell pregnant used to hide the fact. They'd go to Sydney, come back a fair bit thinner and tell everyone they'd been on a diet. But my grandmother was strong-minded. She decided to keep her baby.

After my father was born she met Joe Herbert, whom she married. They had three kids together. But my grandmother gave my father her maiden name—Dromgold. In those days, people looked down on those who brought shame upon their family. But when I think of my grandmother, I can only admire her strength and fortitude.

So Dad lived with his mum and his stepfather. He used to go and stay with his other aunties from time to time. Interestingly, Dad and his half-brother stayed friends. I reckon the stigma of being born illegitimate would have stung him. In my book, that was more than half his problem. You can see how the booze could have helped him forget his origins.

Mind you, he never mentioned that part of his life to me. These days, you'd try and talk about it, but not back then. He never brought it up, and I thought if I asked it would have hurt him more. I guess we'd all just learned to avoid the subject.

Physically, Dad and I shared at least one attribute—we both had a great deal of back hair! He never tried to hide his hairiness and often stripped down to do his physical work—I was more self-conscious.

Sadly, my father's addiction to alcohol affected his relationships in the family and rendered him something of a failure as breadwinner and family protector. He just was not up to those tasks and let us down time after time. Again, luck was on our side because Mum was incredibly capable and we had our Great Uncle John, our saviour. He was the guiding light in my childhood. He lived with us all through my childhood. I left the farm once I had grown up, but he stayed for life.

My mother was a Humphries—her grandfather, aged fourteen, was transported to Australia for seven years for stealing a watch. You'd think that was an unfortunate start to his life, but it was probably the best thing that could have happened to him. I'll tell you a little more about Thomas Horton in a later chapter—not because I'm a history buff, but because it's interesting to see how much influence his character and personality had on the family, even four generations down the track.

The Hortons hailed from the north of England. Mum was raised as a Protestant and converted to Roman Catholicism to marry my father. Dad was a wild lad by all accounts and from an early age adopted the loveable larrikin and rogue persona. I'm sure, to my mother, he was attractive in a bad boy way and that must have disappointed her parents who'd bought her up in rather more refined circumstances and would have hoped she'd marry a solid, good providing, farmer.

It's an old story that's been lived many times: good girl meets and falls in love with bad boy. Girl from an Anglican background and boy a wild Catholic. Most stories stop there and we're left to imagine they lived happily ever after. But for the children of such a marriage, there's no fairy tale ending.

As a child, I can remember that Dad went away to work as a shearer and time and again he returned home without a penny. He was known to be a hard worker and was paid by cheque, cashed the cheque and drank all the cash away. There were even times when he returned home without his bedroll—he had sold it for drink money. When the family went into town once a month, Dad started drinking as soon as he got there, got drunk and stayed drunk for the next three days. He was an embarrassment and behaved like a drunk in public, although he was a placid drunk. He was only in jail once that I know of, for urinating in a public place.

Kangaira tennis club. My grandfather, Edward Humphries, 2nd male from left.

Perhaps as a small child you were unaware of things, but as I grew up I became aware of Uncle John's frustration with Dad and his drinking. Uncle John was not a wowser. He enjoyed a drink when we went into town, although more than once I heard him abuse my father for his drinking and its effect on the family, especially Mum.

Uncle John asked the local priest to find someone to talk to Dad about his drinking but nothing helped and he just kept drinking right up until he died at the age of sixty-two. Everyone, his mother, Mum, the doctors, the priest, his sisters and his children puzzled about how to help him. Of course, as a society we now know much more about addiction than was known in those times. I want to be clear about the impact on the family—he was not a vicious man but when he was drinking that consumed all of the family's money. I am also mindful that it was not all bad—probably approximately eighty-five percent of the time was difficult and the rest was good.

I was four when my younger sister Pauline was born. I don't remember much about her birth, or her coming home. In fact, it would be fair to say that her arrival had little impact on me. That didn't last, and Pauline soon made her presence felt!

By this stage I'd found my place in the family. I idolised my Mum, and looked up to my Dad with equal parts of boyish admiration and fear. I was totally devoted to Uncle John. I'd follow him out into the paddocks, wanting to be just like him when I grew up. I never felt lost or scared or left behind with Uncle John. Sure there were times when I felt cold or hungry, but I knew of nothing different.

When I was younger, we started travelling with my father to his work and lived on site in a tent. We spent two to four weeks at a shearing shed then moved on to the next as the job finished. We returned to our small farm in between jobs. Our mother found that if we were with Dad at the worksite, he doled his pay out to our mother as she needed it and we did not starve. She also worked out that she could get access to his pay while he was drunk, and control the money and she often helped herself to his cash when he was passed out. He would awaken the next morning having no idea about where his money had gone and never made a fuss about it. As Mum was exceptionally good at stretching the money out, that was how we survived. We would be away about three or four months each year.

When we arrived at a shearing shed, Dad selected a camp site away from others and set up camp, pitching the tent. I recall once camping in the Brewarrina area near a huge river and I caught a huge fish which I put back in the river in a sugar bag to keep it fresh until we ate it. I also remember a family that owned a large property on which Dad was working giving our mother meat to cook for us. I do not remember what we ate but we never went hungry. Our toilet during those times was the bush or a hole dug in the ground with a shovel. There were outdoor baths for the shearers that we could use—shearing is dirty work and the shearers were covered in blood, sheep faeces and oil from handling the fleece.

When we were back at our farm, we always had food—rabbits, wild duck, sheep and we grew our own vegetables such as carrots, swede, peas and seasonal vegetables. We always had clothes as Mum could sew and modify clothes to fit us. Our housing was modest—an old slab hut with a partly dirt and partly timber floor, and there was paper stuck to the inside of the slabs with flour and water to seal some of the gaps. We lived in that hut until the mid-fifties. One room had an altar set up in it as my father was very strict about making us attend Mass—even as a youngster I was struck by his hypocrisy and the inconsistency between his stated beliefs and his actual behaviour towards his family.

Most of the kids from Frogmore school about 1941.

Another thing I remember about Dad from childhood was that he was unpredictable. There were times he stuck up for us but also times when he gave us a good beating for no apparent reason. On one occasion he hit me with a two-foot-long broomstick after warning my sister Pat and me as we raced giddily around in a figure-of-eight pattern on our bikes that if we crashed he would hit us. Predictably, we did crash and I got the threatened beating. I thought we should both get the same treatment, but she was not punished. He also kicked me in the bottom (wearing his hobnail boots) hard enough to lift me well off the ground, and ultimately I needed to have an operation for an abscess on my tail bone.

There was one day my sisters Pauline, Patricia and I were walking to school, a distance of about three and half miles, and Pauline was very young and a slow walker. Pat was up ahead, I was in the middle and frustrated with how slowly Pauline was walking and swore at her, telling her to hurry up. I had forgotten that Dad was up the hill setting rabbit traps and heard every word and came after me. He kicked me once, then again, and then with each step I took continued to kick me. It went on for a long time.

Dad was the only driver in the family and we were dependent on him, which went badly on our monthly trip into town. He would get completely drunk, and the family suffered the shame of having to ask people to assist us to get him into the car and after which my sisters and I drove home as best we could. There were times when I operated the brake and accelerator while my sister sat up and steered the car as her feet could not reach the pedals!

Before we were old enough to assist, I remember being at Frogmore at a dance with Mum and Dad. Afterwards the local police office, Jack Sparkes, came up to Mum and said, 'Dick can't sit up let alone drive—come with me and I'll show you how to drive yourselves home.' Poor Mum had a rough lesson from him and then drove us all home.

As we got older, our driving skills came in handy one night, though. Dad was working away, and Mum and Uncle John were away too. It was cracker night with a large bonfire in Boorowa to celebrate the Queen's birthday Pauline and I wanted to go. On the property there was an old Dodge car jacked up near the wood heap. Dad had run a belt around a rear wheel which drove the saw when he needed to chop timber. I managed to get the car off the blocks, get it going and we drove into town to see the bonfire! When we got back, I jacked it back up and reconnected the belt and we got away with that adventure.

Mum needed to regularly visit the doctor in Cowra as she had gall bladder problems. She went to the doctor while Dad went to the hotel and wrote himself off. The drive home was to be dreaded with him at the wheel, especially when the creeks we had to cross were in flood. He placed a bag in front of the car to stop water getting into the distributor and we always knew that, when we crossed, the front wheels would get to dry land but the back wheels were still in water when the car would stop dead. Dad staggered out of the car, pulled car parts off, and dried them out to get the car going while we watched the water rise again. It was terrifying for the children, but we survived.

Looking back, these were hard times but you just got through it. I still loved Dad. He taught me that I wanted to be a loving and protective father who provided well for his family. I really think I learned about failure from him—he failed his family. As a consequence, I developed a strong desire to avoid failure!

I also learned from him an ability to innovate—like the time he decided to put a new set of rings in the old Ford motor car—like most people at that time he was a bush mechanic. So he did the job, then both parents and all four kids pushed the car to get it started. It started all right, to our relief, then promptly burst into flames—the rings were too tight. So it was all hands into the sand and dirt to throw onto the fire to extinguish it!

There was a similar occasion when the A Model Ford broke its cross spring. Dad ordered a new one in the mail but when it arrived it did not fit. Once again, the family were deployed to load the back of the car with football sized rocks to force the ill-fitting spring into place. He turned his hand to many things; the isolation and lack of money meant he had to innovate. I learned that from him—that resourcefulness. It certainly paid off for me in my later years.

I was surprised by my grief when he died. I was a pallbearer and as we carried him out of church I burst into tears—I was overcome by memories of the bad times. All of us just kept forgiving him all the way through. I kick myself now because we looked after him until he died—we took meals to him and I always took him a bottle of beer to have with his meals, thinking that was the right thing. I have since been told that was the worst thing I could have done.

On the other hand, there was my incredibly capable mother, trying to protect us from the worst of my father's behaviour and doing all the hard work, with Uncle John's backing, to raise us.

Joan, my youngest sister arrived when I was five. Her arrival marked a change for me. It became very clear that boys and girls were treated very differently. I was moved onto the verandah to sleep—although *verandah* is a very grand word for a very basic shelter at the front of the house. I was suddenly expected to do more with the men and less around the house. I cut and carried wood, hunted rabbits, and learned to ride a horse. I also went on bivouacs with the guys when they were working away from the farm. They worked away a lot. Our farm wasn't good grazing or growing country, so like Irish people the world over, the men used their muscle and brawn labouring for others. That's never a path to riches but it kept the family fed. I remember hunting, riding, hanging around shearing sheds and generally learning how to be one of the men.

Perhaps it was my mother's influence, but I started a dream

of a different life—a life where I prospered, rather than just surviving. I started to be aware of other people in the district, aware of how they looked at us, what they thought of us and how they reacted to us. A pride and determination was born in me to be and do differently.

As a child, I adored Mum. She was the rock upon whom we all depended and looked after all of us wonderfully well, including Dad. As they got older and Dad did less paid work, she travelled with him and cooked for the shearers and rouseabouts to earn an income. There could be fifteen shearers and she could be cooking for twenty-five people.

Mum was willing to tackle anything. At one time we had a Hupmobile Eight car and she singlehandedly worked out how to make a canvas hood for it, with celluloid windows she cut and sewed in. After she had made the hood, she worked out a way to waterproof and blacken it and it really set the car off beautifully. She also looked after Dad lovingly—she groomed him and dressed him up and he went into town looking like a million dollars, despite all the grief he must have given her over the years. After he died, she took on work in a factory in Sydney.

Mum inherited some money after her mother, who was a really tough woman, passed away. Mum bought a home in Frogmore for 1200 pounds, although the law or convention at the time meant she had to place it in Dad's name. There were times though when we did not live there. We lived in a shed at Uncle John's farm, Fern Hill until Dad organised himself to remove and rebuild the three-bedroom house from Frogmore.

This was a major project, and he approached it in a novel way. He cut it into sections. God knows where he got the idea from—came out of his own head, most likely. He cut into the walls, cut through the corners, lifted the iron off the roof and took the rafters down. He only had hand tools: a timber saw and a hacksaw. I was around twelve years old and I worked as his assistant. Not that I was strong enough to cut the house up. I helped him lay the walls down and load them on a truck. The house was weatherboards inside and out, framed with radiata pine, so it wasn't too heavy.

Plan of Fern Hill Farm – outlined in red.

We spent one or two weeks cutting it up, travelling in from the farm each day. The weather was stinking hot. He always took his packed lunch in his tuckerbox. Cooked meat and bread, with butter running everywhere with the heat. Everyone reckoned he was a nutcase. Mum had begged him to sell the house and we'll build something smaller out on the farm, which made a hell of a lot more sense.

So we trucked the pieces down to Fern Hill and unloaded them, before Dad lost interest in the project. He'd already pulled down the old slab hut on the farm, leaving only an old corrugated iron building. The house from Frogmore lay in pieces on the ground for some years. In the end, it fell to Mum and me with the help of a bush carpenter to cut a hole in the side of the corrugated iron building and set up a bathroom in it. Mum and I installed a large cast iron bath and hand basin, and a chip heater. I recall Mum having to finish the brickwork for the chimney!

Me, Jack Elkins & Pat in front. Pauline, Joan & Roma
Good on Silvy the mare. And Hirachi the foal.

Before we occupied our new home, Mum managed to look after all of us (Dad when he was home, my sisters Pat, Pauline, Joan, me and Uncle John) in that simple shed. There was another baby, Mary, who died at birth—life must have been very hard for Mum at times.

Me, Pat, Mum, Joan & Pauline the day Pat & Pauline went to board at Binalong.

Mum cooked in a camp oven over an open fire with the size of the fire regulating the temperature of the fire. Dripping was used for all cooking and we children loved making ourselves dripping sandwiches! Our meals included corned lamb, and baked dinners. Of course there was no reliable refrigeration—they killed a sheep, usually once a week, salted the meat to preserve it and then hung it. The "refrigerator" was a metal safe with small holes perforated in it that were too small for blowflies to fly through, and hessian around the base of it so the bottom of the hessian sat in a trough of water. The water soaked up through the hessian and the breeze kept the contents cool.

Although we had none of the modern conveniences taken for granted now, we had a wireless which ran off a wet cell battery. It needed to be taken into town for charging at regular intervals, so we could only listen to the news for half-an-hour each evening. We listened to the news and always got the prices being paid for rabbit skins. We also had a gramophone and our seventy-eight records and we had a piano, a guitar, piano accordion, mouth organ and flute and made our own music.

Around home Dad dressed in straggly clothes, like a farmer. Half the time he went unshaven. A lot of the bush people were the same. He was a pretty savage looking hombre. His brown hair was so dark it was almost black.

Maybe once a month he'd get the itch to head into town. Mum would get him all mockered up and dressed to the nines. He'd take a bath and shave off three weeks' worth of beard. If Mum found any marks or stains on his clothes she'd clean them off with cold tea and salt. They'd be spots left over from his last trip into town. Then Mum would press his suit. You could just about cut yourself on the creases of his trousers. He usually wore a dark suit, although there was one suit I grew out of and handed down to him. It was a light grey with a fine stripe. That was the only time he wore a lighter suit.

Then he'd go out and fire up the car. The car had a crank handle on the front to turn the motor. You had to fold your thumb out of the way so if it kicked or backfired it wouldn't break your thumb. That's how I remember Dad heading off to town, all spruced up in his tie and suit and his smartly buffed shoes. He looked immaculate—at least until he hit town and got on the piss. Then he didn't give a stuff. When he got drunk he was useless. Hopeless.

Uncle John gave him a good talking-to once. 'You're a smart looking man, Dick,' he said. 'Why don't you wake up to yourself? When you're sober you wouldn't piss on them bastards that's laughing at you.'

Like all the women around our way Mum was very casual in her dress. She'd get dressed up to go to town with Dad.

But on a normal working day, she would be up in the sheep yard pushing the sheep up, or in the kitchen cooking dinner. If the shearing was on she'd be baking scones and cakes for morning and afternoon tea, and making lunch for the shearers. We supplied them with meals in those days.

It was a significant occasion when we were connected to the telephone when I was in my late teens. Uncle John and I cut the posts from timber standing on the farm, dug the holes for them and installed them so that the telephone could be connected to the home. It was a party line with five connections but only one party could be on the line at a time. We each had our own ring code but there was no privacy because anyone else could listen in on the conversation. I recall that there were two people talking on the line and as they ended the call they said good night to each other and good night to the eavesdropping operator who breezily replied with her own good night to each of them!

Mum baked all our bread—I helped her knead it and she baked about four loaves at a time twice each week.

Beef was a rare treat in winter and we had it occasionally when local families pooled their resources to kill a beast with the cost and the meat shared between the families. I recently saw a documentary on the Amish way of life and watching it was like reliving my childhood.

When I was about ten years old, we kept about eight cows and I milked them. Mum separated the milk to make our own butter. I used to help Mum beat the cream. I hated the taste of our homemade butter. One of my happiest experiences was the discovery of "town" butter when I was about fourteen years old. I rode my bike into Boorowa, about an hour-long ride over corrugated dirt roads. At Ryan's bakery. I bought a freshly baked "married loaf" and one quarter of a pound of butter and stuffed the butter into the centre of the warm loaf and ate the bread and butter with butter oozing all over my chin.

I still love the taste of butter on fresh bread—it has done me no apparent harm as I have no cholesterol issues. Only one of my four siblings has a cholesterol problem. I reflect sometimes on how different food these days often tastes—I cannot find a sausage that I like. When I was a child and we killed a sheep, it was always a hogget (i.e. a fully grown sheep with a full mouth of teeth. Nothing was wasted—the cold meat left over would be minced by Mum in her mincer on the side of the kitchen table into mince for shepherd's pie and similar meals. Fertilizer was only used on the farm for the wheat, not on any other crop. We grew lucerne to feed the chooks, hay to be stored as feed for cattle and horses if there was insufficient.

Del at 10 years old - the picture that started it all!!

At times, great amusement arose at Fern Hill when visitors came to the property. The house was built on the flat top of a hill with shearing shed behind it. There was a perimeter fence to keep the stock out of the house yard and so visitors frequently parked their cars on the slope outside the perimeter fence. Hand brakes were not always reliable in those days and great hilarity occurred as visitors said their good- byes and moved towards where they had left their car, only to discover that the brake had failed and the car had rolled back downhill and was down in the paddock!

When I was a kid our house was full of music and I loved all that jamming and singing. We had a couple of pianos in the living room. One was out of tune, but the other was a steel-framed Beale, supposed to be one of the top pianos. Uncle John brought it for my two youngest sisters so they could learn to play. The nuns up at the convent were supposed to teach them but they never really got the knack.

On top of the Beale was Uncle Kevin's wedding photo. Uncle Kevin was eight years older than me. Irene, his wife, was another seven years older than him. She should have been had up for baby snatching! Irene was a gorgeous looking woman, a lovely personality. When I was thirteen or fourteen I looked at this photo, pointed out the flower girl standing beside the happy couple, and announced that I would marry her one day. I said it more than once, apparently. Not that I ever thought I'd meet her. Was she my dream girl? Absolutely. I've still got that wedding photo, too.

As well as the pianos we had all types of musical instruments in the house. A violin, a mouth organ, a piano accordion. When Uncle Teddy came to visit he'd bring his violin and a couple of longneck bottles of beer and before you knew he'd be plucking that violin like a banjo and we'd all be singing along. I was brought up with Irish music.

Uncle Ted was married to Mum's sister. Mum and he used to play at dances in local villages. If the woman who usually played couldn't make it they'd get up on stage and he'd have those violin strings sizzling. Mum played by ear. She could hear a song on the radio then go and play in on the piano. I tried to play everything known to man but no matter how much I loved the music it never loved me back. Thing is, I'm tone deaf.

Mum did her best to teach me. She wrote the notes on the keyboard and I was supposed to follow along. Must have surprised her that I didn't share her talent. The best I could do was pick out 'God Save the Queen'. Funny sort of song for an Irish boy to be playing, but Mum had converted from the Church of England. We were always taught respect. We were brought up to call people Mister or Missus or Doctor. If you didn't you'd cop a walloping.

CHAPTER TWO

Thomas Horton

It's pretty obvious that my mother was a strong woman. Where did her strength come from? I'm going to tell you what I know of Thomas Horton, my great grandfather on my mother's side. When I was a kid I had no interest in my family history. As I grew older, I began to wonder about my ancestry. I'm sharing the story of Thomas Horton for two reasons. One, it's an interesting tale which reveals a lot about the early days of New South Wales. Two, it shows the sense of character which has come down through the Horton line, and which continues now with the Dromgolds.

Thomas Horton arrived in Australia at the age of fifteen. You couldn't say he was an enthusiastic emigrant. Thomas was born in Warwickshire in 1820. By the early 1830s the north of England was embroiled in political conflict. The Reform Act of 1832 gave property owners the right to vote, but the working poor remained disenfranchised. And young Thomas had strong working class roots.

He worked as a brass founder's boy—dangerous work which left him with a prominent scar on his left thumb. It also gave him a taste for more exotic metals, which might explain why on 4 August 1835 he was hauled before the Warwick quarter sessions. He had been charged with pickpocketing a gold watch valued at three pounds and stealing a steel chain valued at three shillings, the property of one Henry Wade. His older brother William, aged 16, was his co-accused.

Although Thomas pleaded not guilty, the judge found otherwise, and sentenced him to seven years' imprisonment, with transportation to New South Wales thrown in for good measure. William was given six months' hard labour, and two private floggings. Apparently, the judge considered Thomas to be a corrupting influence on his older brother, and not without reason. This wasn't Thomas's first brush with the law. He'd previously served six months for unknown crimes. Given the sentence imposed on William, you would suspect that Thomas had received a flogging or two as well.

Apart from his scar, Thomas is described as standing four feet eight and a half inches tall, with chestnut eyes and a dark pale complexion. He apparently never attended school. However, there was a note on his transportation papers describing him as a bright boy who could read and write. While it's easy to condemn Thomas as a thief, the odds were stacked against him from the start. As an indication of the prevailing attitudes at the time, it's worth remembering that the government had generously reduced the maximum working hours for children as young as nine to thirteen hours a day, six days per week!

So Thomas was marched aboard the convict ship *Moffatt* for the 13,000 mile journey to Australia, knowing he would never return to the country of his birth. There is no record of Thomas visiting the ship's surgeon during the voyage, so his journey must have been relatively uneventful—apart from being packed into a crowded bunkroom with four hundred other convicts, some of them no doubt hardened criminals. When the *Moffatt* entered Sydney Harbour it was blown onto the rocks at North Head, and narrowly avoided being wrecked. After such last-minute drama, Thomas's life was about to take a turn for the better.

Once ashore, he was taken to the Hyde Park Barracks, where he was assigned to the service of Francis Forbes, the Chief Justice of the Supreme Court of New South Wales. Given Thomas's experiences with the law, you might expect him to have been wary. However, Forbes was a fair and principled man. He had clashed with the previous Governor, Sir Ralph Darling, over Darling's plans to restrict the liberty of the press. While Forbes had prevailed, the conflict with Darling had continued until Darling was replaced in 1831.

Forbes had also pushed for self-government in New South Wales, an end to the transportation of convicts, and the right to trial by jury in the colony. Thomas Horton worked on the properties owned by Sir Francis and his brother at Muswellbrook, in the Upper Hunter Region. He also accompanied Sir Francis on a number of business journeys through New South Wales. Forbes died in his home in Newtown, Sydney, in 1841, at the relatively young age of 57 years. His heavy workload and Darling's harassment had taken their toll.

Before his death, Forbes had arranged one final favour for Thomas Horton. He completed the paperwork necessary for Thomas to receive his ticket of leave, along with permission to remain in Muswellbrook. On 4 September 1842 Thomas was granted his freedom, having served out his sentence.

There is little evidence of Thomas's activities over the next twelve years. On 23 November 1849, he was granted fifty acres of land near Boorowa in New South Wales. This property became known as Horton's Hill.

On 2 February 1853, he married Lucy Ovens of Bigga, New South Wales, the daughter of Thomas and Mary

Ovens. Thomas Ovens was a former convict who had been transported for seven years for theft.

After their wedding, Thomas and Lucy departed for the goldfields of Yackandandah, in Northern Victoria. Their son William, known as Digger, was born there. However, conditions in the goldfields were not suitable for a young family, so they soon returned to Bigga, where William was baptised. The next five children were born at Horton's Hill, and over the following years Thomas bought and traded many blocks of land in the area. In 1874 he sold Horton's Hill to Patrick Hogan, another great grandfather of mine. When you look at the records, you realise that both my great grandfathers on my mother's side were living at Horton's Hill at the same time.

Over the years Thomas had a few more brushes with the law. In 1867 Samual Tyhurst was charged with slaughtering a bullock carrying Thomas Horton's brand, a half-circle containing the initials 'TH'. While Tyhurst admitted to shooting the bullock, he explained that he was hungry, and thought the bullock was wild. His testimony was undermined by the fact that he had taken an effort to conceal the hide in a hollowed-out tree, where Thomas found it.

The magistrate sentenced Tyhurst to two years' hard labour. Hoping to avoid hard labour, Tyhurst argued he should be sent to Goulburn Gaol, where he could do his time soft. Unconvinced, the magistrate ordered him to serve his sentence in Darlinghurst, suggesting he would get plenty of exercise there!

Thomas's next court case saw him appear in the Boorowa Licencing Court on a charge of supplying two glasses of rum to one John Gleeson, on a Sunday no less! Thomas provided witnesses who swore otherwise, but he was found guilty nonetheless. It's worth noting that the informant received half of the thirty pound fine imposed.

Finally, there is a document found at the police station at Frogmore, stating that Dennis Walsh and Thomas Horton had settled their disagreement out of court, and asking that the case be struck from the court's roll. The nature of the dispute is unclear, and the spelling, evidence of both men's lack of schooling.

All in all, Elizabeth bore ten children, and passed away in 1900. To me, Thomas and Elizabeth were both pioneers in the truest sense of the word. I imagine Thomas turning his hand to anything that would earn a quid, from rabbiting to shearing to farming to gold mining. He had a good eye for property, buying and selling blocks of land in the Boorowa district. He and Elizabeth worked hard, and during the course of their lives built a strong base of the family's fortunes. By the end of his life, he had bought a farm for each of his six children.

However, what takes a lifetime to build can be lost in a flash. Thomas's youngest son, the one who inherited the family home, went bad. He started importing American cars but the business failed, and he ended up with nothing. He became so desperate he burned one of his cars for the insurance money. This must have emboldened him, because he then set fire to the family home—the original homestead Thomas Horton built on Old Man Gunyah Creek—and claimed the insurance.

So it's a fair bet to say the Horton's weren't all angels. My father's family bought Horton's Hill, and my father ended up with about a quarter of the original run. The tennis court and the cricket pitch - of which we'll hear more later - were both on Horton's former property.

CHAPTER THREE

Uncle John

Uncle John was a unique person—he was father, grandfather and mentor to me. If he had not been there, my sisters and I would probably have been taken away from our parents and put into an orphanage.

He taught me to be generous. He went into town once or twice every couple of months and without fail he returned with two shillings' worth of lollies for us—a huge bag which we devoured greedily. Those were precious moments he gave us when we did not feel poor—we knew that some of the families around us looked down on us, probably because of Dad.

Uncle John had inherited the farm, Fern Hill, a holding of about 353 acres, which had originally been taken up as a selection by his mother. He remained a bachelor all of his life. He worked hard on the property and improved it continually.

Physically, he was short, but he was fit and athletic as farmers were in those days because they had to work hard physically. He walked all over his property, always accompanied by two or three dogs and carrying a mattock over his shoulder. He always wore sandshoes without socks, a hat, and a suit coat around the farm as he worked. He constantly smoked a pipe and checked his sheep every day. He had thick bushy hair, which he had me cut for him with hand clippers between his visits to the barber. I never saw him use anything but his fingers to tame his wild hair. As he got older and had to have dental work, he had extracted teeth filled or replaced with gold—which was unusual at that time. As children, we were fascinated by the flash of gold in his mouth.

One time when I was four or five I had a bad case of the hiccups. There was a story going around that if someone told you a lie, the hiccups would stop. When I told my great aunt that I had hiccups, she said, 'Go and ask Uncle John to tell you a lie.'

So I did. He looked at me with his gold-toothed grin. "Of course I can,' he said.

'What is it, John?'

'That you're a bloody good boy!'

He and his sisters laughed about it for years. There were only three in the family: Babe, Wig, and John. His sister was one of my grandmothers.

Uncle John.

One of the great pleasures we had at Fern Hill was swimming, or pretending to swim, in the local creek which adjoined the property. There was a beautiful swimming hole there—crystal clear water and willows overhanging the creek. In fact, Uncle John did not bath at home, He headed down to the creek with a cake of soap, stripped off and bathed in the creek.

One day, Uncle John and I had been at the creek "swimming" (he taught us to dogpaddle and we thought we could swim) and were heading back home when he saw a black snake in the bulrushes near us. He always carried a mattock with him about the farm but on this occasion he was carrying a tomahawk instead and as he stepped forward to kill it with his tomahawk the bulrushes gave way beneath him and he crashed into the creek with a great cry! Seconds later he resurfaced coughing and spluttering. That snake had a lucky escape!

Uncle John took me to the Royal Easter Show a few times—these were very special journeys for me. We went to all the exhibits including the night events and then we would walk up William Street to admire the MG cars for him and motor bikes for me. On one occasion he actually ordered an MG car for himself to come all the way from England—it had to be red! When it finally arrived, it was a fawn colour and he refused to take delivery. He stood his ground and insisted on the red colour, which subsequently arrived. I wonder now whether they just repainted the fawn car, but he was happy. He was probably in his sixties by then.

Uncle John also had an uncanny ability to select dresses and coats for girls. During our trips to Sydney, he chose clothes for my three sisters and for the two Evans girls who lived on a nearby property and when we brought them home the clothes always fitted! He had no measurements—he would just hold the garments up and assess them.

He had a temper when aroused—I remember Uncle John abusing Dad about his drinking and he also had a tense relationship with a neighbour, Mr. Sol Cooper. He and Mr. Cooper would stand shouting at each other over the fence, waving their pliers furiously at each other arguing about the repair of the shared floodgate.

One day, Mr. Cooper bellowed at Uncle John, complaining that one of our cows had come onto his property and demanding its immediate removal! In response Uncle John sent my friend Jack and me into Mr. Cooper's to get the cow. We had ridden in, successfully rounded up the cow and driven it back, when Jack's saddle got caught up on the floodgate. At the same time, we realised that Mr. Cooper was rushing towards us raging, bellowing and demanding to know what we were up to on his land. Uncle John quickly ducked under the floodgate and met Mr. Cooper on his land, where they had a fierce argument. I heard Uncle John telling Mr. Cooper 'not to carry on like a mug'. Mr. Cooper was Uncle John's opposite—he was as mean as Uncle John was generous. Uncle John was well regarded by the local people; Mr. Cooper was universally disliked.

When I was maybe five years old, Uncle John told us a story about going in an aeroplane which crashed, leaving him uninjured but with no fondness for aeroplanes! He used to visit Sydney for the Royal Easter Show. This particular year he decided to go for a joyride out at the airfield. They got about fifty feet up into the air before they crashed into another plane. I don't know what sort of plane it was—

something like a Tiger Moth, all fabric and wires. The two planes came down jumbled together and landed in a heap. Uncle John's plane landed tail-first. Luckily, it didn't catch fire. He walked away with only a few scratches.

While I could never find anything in the newspapers about this incident, it was apparently on the radio, so it's a true story. After that, I hated aeroplanes. If I heard one flying over the house I'd take my .22 and draw a bead on it. I wouldn't have shot at one and if I had, I certainly wouldn't have hit it. But I attribute my fear of airplanes, which I've had all of my life, to that experience of his.

When I visited Sydney with Uncle John he took me to more than just the Royal Easter Show. Bob Dyer and Jack Davey were on the radio back then, and Uncle John loved to go and sit in the live audience. I'd go with him, and it was fantastic watching them making these programs—quiz shows and so forth. We'd be clapping and carrying on. Uncle John had no worries poking about the town and introducing you to new and exciting things.

He'd take me out to dinner at Ling Nams, the best Chinese restaurant in town. I'd get all mockered up and feel on top of the world. Afterwards, I'd head home and Uncle John would disappear off into the night, reappearing mysteriously at the boarding house some time later. He never talked about what he's been up to. This is one of the questions I thought about it more later in life—where did he disappear to?

There was one time when he went to visit a lady he knew up in Kings Cross. He told me to wait outside while he went in and spoke with her. He wasn't too definite about the subject of this supposed conversation. So I waited outside and twenty minutes later out he came, looking like a cat who'd just lapped up a saucer of cream. Of course, I was only

Uncle John with his Niece Pat Humphries.

a young fella, so I had no idea. It's only later that I put two and two together.

Uncle John loved my mother as if she was his own daughter and was deeply troubled by my father's drinking and apparent disregard for his responsibility as breadwinner, husband and father. We were so lucky to have him in our lives. When he died, he left his property to me in the place of my father as he knew Dad would squander it. I used the sale proceeds to make sure that Mum owned her own home until the end of her life.

I went to visit Uncle John in Young Hospital one time when he was recovering from surgery. He greeted me, then told me the man in the next bed was my paternal grandfather, Richard Platt. Let me tell you—that was weird. It was a large ward, with fourteen beds or so lined around the walls. And there, in the bed beside Uncle John's, was this man we both hated. The man who'd chosen to marry another woman, leaving my father with the stigma of being born out-of-wedlock.

Anyone watching me would have seen the blood rushing to my face. To this day I can't remember what he looked like because I never so much as laid eyes on him, I was livid. I'd never met him, no one had ever talked about him. I thought he was the source of so many problems in our family, of Dad hitting the bottle the way he did. So I'd be damned if I was going to so much as glance his way.

'Stuff you,' I thought. Mind you, he did a bit of stuffing himself, getting two girls pregnant at the one time. I couldn't wait to get out of there. To this day I have no idea why my grandfather was in hospital. The red mist came down, and I was gone.

Being so angry meant I lost the opportunity to speak with him. If I had my time again I'd do things differently now. There's so much I could have asked him. For all his sins, he's my blood. But that's all water under the bridge. Uncle John never mentioned him again.

I have referred above to my dear friend Jack—I now would like to share a little more about him...

CHAPTER FOUR

Jack Elkins

During the war, Uncle John had leased the neighbouring property owned by the Elkins family who had moved into Yass so their daughters could attend school there. The Elkins family and the other large landholders such as the Roberts and Croker families were wealthy - not like us.

Jack's father stayed at our house for a couple of weeks at a time and one week end he took me home to his house and that was when I first met Jack. Jack was always cracking jokes—good-humoured, friendly, and we got on like a house on fire

The place they lived in was the scene of one of the more embarrassing events of my life. It was an old shop building with the shop at the front and the residence out the back. I remember getting up in the night to go to the toilet. I went to the door to urinate outside but with horror realized I was peeing into a window as the urine splashed back at me and pooled at my feet, making a hell of a mess! I woke Jack up and asked for something to mop it up with—I was so embarrassed. Because I normally slept on the verandah at Fern Hill, I was used to getting out of bed and walking to the edge of the verandah and peeing. The girls though had a pot but the boys just peed outside. I remember being really mortified by my error!

My first impression of Jack was that I could trust him—we

Jack Elkins, dog & me.

could get up to mischief together and you knew he'd never dob, although his father managed to extract a confession out of him once. When we were about twelve, we stole some tobacco from his neighbour—we were so naïve that we overlooked the fact that our bike tracks could be clearly seen in the dusty road riding from our home to their paddock, travelling a mile into the neighbour's house block and back out again! We knew the tobacco was in the house and no one locked their home in those days. As it turned out, we hid the tobacco under a nearby culvert to come back to later and smoke but it rained heavily that night and was washed away so we never got to enjoy it!

At first we completely denied any involvement but Jack's father was at him for years to admit he had taken the tobacco and finally years later, when Jack was about sixteen, Jack's father tackled him again about it but this time got Jack down on the ground and held a reaping hook at his neck and threatened 'I'll bloody kill you if you don't tell me the truth about that tobacco.' Jack confessed all, took a serious flogging from his father as punishment and immediately came to see me to tell me—he was very disappointed in himself for letting me down, as he put it. He was, throughout his life, a true-blue sort of bloke. I received a stern lecture from Uncle John, which was completely justified. I remain appalled at what we did and it was wrong to bring such shame on my Uncle.

We got up to other mischief but nothing serious. I was eighteen months older than Jack—I remember joyriding with him. They were building a shearing shed at their place and the construction workers left the utility there with the keys in it after they had gone home and so we jumped in and burned around the paddock together.

We both became proficient horse riders. We had draft horses on the property which were used to pull the two-furrowed plough for the family vegetable patch. They were strong, slow moving beasts. We rode our ponies hard and would chase the draft horse brumbies around over cattle grids which our ponies could jump! We once drove a mob of cattle about thirty miles by ourselves—with me the thirteen-year-old in charge!

I remember breaking my first horse. I got him into a ploughed paddock, so he couldn't get a grip. Jack, Keith and another mate were there. I nearly pissed myself getting on that horse. It pig-rooted, then I rode off like a champion. I was bloody petrified but I did not let on. You couldn't let your mates see your fear.

My sister Joan and I went for a ride one day. I was about 17, she would have been 13 or so. I'd just broken a young horse, and I put Joan on its dam, a sprightly old mare. We came to a little watercourse across the road, just a foot wide, and the mare jumped it. Not a massive leap, but it caught Joan unawares, and she tumbled off backwards. Fortunately, she landed somewhere soft. I reached down, cowboy style, grabbed hold of her, and said 'Climb up behind me.' It's a wonder my horse didn't buck its head off. It seemed settled enough, so I just put Joan up behind me and away we went.

When we arrived home Mum blew her top when she heard our story. 'Fancy putting young Joan on a horse you've just broken! What were you thinking?' Truth is, I wasn't thinking at all, and we both arrived home safely. I reckon a horse knows when you've mastered it and does what it's told. I didn't think anything of it when Joan fell of the horse, either. You grew up tough back then.

Jack's family's property was a large holding and they cleared a lot of the timber on it by chopping it down so that stumps remained. Our fun came when I jumped on the largest tractor we had and Jack jumped on the Ferguson tractor and with a heavy chain dragged between the two tractors we removed the stumps in some sections.

I remember a time when Jack and I had gathered up some dead wool in a chaff bag to sell. We left it near a large tree to come back later to collect. Unfortunately for us, Uncle John told my sister Pat about it and she, with Jack's older sister Faye, went and grabbed it, sold the wool and with the proceeds they each bought a box brownie camera, which I understand they both still have! At least we had photos to remind us of the wool...

We had such a lot of freedom ranging over the two properties and having adventures like swimming in the water hole with our ponies, with us clutching their manes for dear life because we actually could not swim. We also learned the farmer's way of being very resourceful and innovative. We had to solve our problems ourselves, then fabricate whatever was needed. After he went to boarding school in secondary school our friendship and adventures were limited to school holidays but our close friendship was not affected in any way.

We had great fun standing on the backs of our ponies and carving words as high up the trunk of the tree as we could reach with our tomahawks! We were trying to convince people that giants were real. When I think of it now, the pony just had to move and we could have had nasty falls with the tomahawk inflicting serious injury. We were lucky. Our parents did not have to worry about us because we looked out for each other.

I remember Jack came to Sydney once with me when I had borrowed Uncle John's MG. He bought a new cigarette lighter but it had no lighter fuel with it. I refueled the MG and drove it abruptly up over the curb, thereby spilling some fuel which went straight into the lighter! It soon emerged that not having a reliable cigarette lighter was pretty irrelevant in an open topped car!

Jack got married two-and-a-half years after I did. I never got an invitation to his wedding. He apologised later. But Jack and his wife were good friends. Margaret now lives not far from us in Canberra.

I knew Margaret long before Jack did. She was about the same age as him. Because her parents had little farm out towards Cowra, she boarded in town in Boorowa. She lived next door to a shop we used to visit on the way out of town. It was a country shop that sold vegetables and farm supplies, they had a café of sorts as well. So we used to see her a lot, but I always thought she never liked me. You know how you get that feeling about people? She never talked much, but that's just her. She never talked much.

Some years ago, when Jack and I had not seen each other for some time, I arrived at my grandson Tom's rugby union match to watch him play. As I approached, I recognised Jack standing on the sideline, watching his grandson Mick playing. I stood quietly beside him and then leaned over and enquired of him 'Do you understand this game mate?' He looked at me, recognised me and said 'No mate, I really don't. They get the ball and they kick it'. It was great to catch up with him and his grandson.

Jack and I remained best friends although our lives took us in different directions but we stayed in touch. He was best man at our wedding and when he was dying I visited him almost every day in palliative care and we relived the fun of our childhood years. His family, including his sister Faye, laughed long and loud at his bedside as we swapped tales.

I found it difficult to watch him die slowly and painfully, he suffered a great deal. I was at his bedside when they gave him his final injection of morphine. I will always remember the dreadful moment when his daughter came out to me saying' You were his best friend'. I had to take off up the corridor and could not speak, it was still a shock that he had died as I thought, or hoped, it would not happen.

Having watched people suffer before dying, I am of the view that a competent adult should be able to choose death. I support euthanasia.

CHAPTER FIVE

School and WW2

The second world war started before I turned five. My father tried to enlist but as a shearer he was classified as an essential worker so he did not serve. There were no treats in those years, we just got simple food. My mother made our butter and bread so the only products we had to buy were flour and sugar. We continued to grow the vegetables described earlier. Clothes and petrol were severely limited.

They'd hold recruitment drives in the bush. They might start somewhere 40 miles out of Boorowa, march along to a drum beat, flags flying, and all the young fellas would be carried away in the excitement and fall in behind. They'd imagine going over to Greece with a rifle and blazing away at the enemy. Never thought for a moment the enemy might be firing back with something bigger, and there was a good chance they'd be killed.

I remember watching them marching past our house at Frogmore. We'd be standing out the front, me and my Mum and my sisters and Dad if he was home. They'd be yelling *g'day* to us and we'd be yelling *g'day* right back at them. Made us feel like we were part of the bloody war. All good fun traipsing through the bush, but it turned into murder once they arrived at the battlefront overseas.

Once they arrived in town they'd line up and enlist. Some of them were underage, but the authorities turned a blind eye. You'd have 16-year-olds signing their lives away. They'd be born in Cowra or Young or Boorowa, and all the nooks and hollows in between, so they'd be on record if anyone wanted to check. Unless it was a home birth or something. No one bothered. Thanks for your signature. Now here's your passport to adventure, mayhem, bloodshed, and possibly, death. Not that you have any say in the outcome.

During the war, food and petrol were rationed but it didn't affect us too much. Even though we were poor we had meat, eggs, potatoes, and plenty of milk. We'd milk the cows, then separate the cream ourselves. I still have a hand-turned separator in the shed. Mum used to bake our bread at home. But when you're young you just want lollies and cakes. After the war the rationing continued through to 1947 or 1950, depending on the item. Tea, sugar and flour were still restricted, but at least the farm provided us with the basics.

As a result, we had an abundance of healthy food. We were never going to starve, even though there were plenty of people around the world picking the crumbs off their table, trying to survive. Sugar was hard to get because it was heavily rationed. We gave up sugar in our tea, and never went back to it. To this day neither my older sister, my younger sister, or me, take sugar in tea. All because of rationing.

Petrol was rationed too, of course. They started making petrol out of wheat in Cowra during the war. I don't know how that turned out—it may not have been a success. Dad used to mix some kerosene with the petrol to make it go further. It's a wonder we weren't blown up.

Mum had gallstone troubles from her early years, so her doctor would sign a form and she'd be given ration coupons for petrol, so she could drive to Young to see a specialist.

I remember the Japanese prisoner of war camp at Cowra, which was fifty miles from our home and the shock that ran through the community after the breakout attempt there which resulted in 231 Japanese deaths, 108 wounded and four Australian deaths. I was terrified by the breakout as it was so close to home—one or two were found dead on properties in our locality. We heard the Prime Minister Mr Curtain on the radio describe the breakout as 'a suicidal disregard for life'.

I was only ten when the Second World War came to an end, so I don't remember all the details of the different battles. We'd all huddle around the battery-powered radio and listen to the news. You had to be quiet; if you made a noise you'd get a kick in the arse. I remember Pearl Harbour being blown up, and the soldiers going ashore at Normandy. Those were big moments, but most of the time as far as the news was concerned, the Australian soldiers were the only ones fighting in the war.

Eventually Dad got a local mechanic to run low voltage electricity through the house, to power a wireless. We needed a special wireless that could run off a 12 volt system. But that was after the war had finished.

The end of the war was memorable, of course. For me, the war ended on the fifteenth of August 1945, when the Japanese surrendered. They seemed like the biggest threat to us. The Germans weren't such a worry. V-J Day is as fresh in my memory as if it happened yesterday. I was ten years old. The surrender was announced to us at Clonalton school and we were released early from school to sing and dance our way home waving wattle at the goannas on our long walk home. Clonalton was the school we attended for four years as it was three and a half miles from the property where Dad worked during that period.

I was twelve years old when it was decided that my sisters would attend the convent as boarders. I remember two of my sisters almost died when they staged their escape from boarding school, located at Binalong. Soon after their arrival, my older sister Pat decided that our younger sister Pauline, a redhead, was being bullied by the nuns and they should run away. Unfortunately, they chose the coldest night of the year to escape and they were found in the early hours of the morning almost dead from exposure. Pat was fourteen and Pauline eight. At least they were smart and followed the railway line, which was how the search party found them after they had travelled about ten miles.

Before my sisters went to boarding school, my schooling was erratic. I started school aged six at Frogmore with my sister Pat who was then eight. That was after the family moved into Frogmore because the farm was too far from a school. However, over the course of the next eight or so years I changed school about ten times, so my education was piecemeal. I spent time with Mum and Dad attending a local school and then, because I missed Uncle John and the farm, I would move back to live at Fern Hill with Uncle John for a few months. Of course, then I missed Mum and Dad and returned to them and changed school again!

When I stayed at Uncle John's, my ride to school was just under five miles each way and when we all lived at Uncle John's we took a so-called 'bus' thirteen-and-a-half miles to Boorowa. The bus was actually a one-and-a-half ton utility with a frame around it. We climbed up the stairs and sat around three sides of it. I was sitting there one day looking out the side when we were about half way to town and I saw a wheel go past us. As I sat there wondering where it came from there was a slow drop as the driver braked—the wheel had literally come off the bus!

The passengers got a slight jolt but no one was injured. Jacky Boyd was the bus driver and he got us to school safely, but late, which was fun for us. Once we reached Boorowa, my sisters went to the Catholic school and I went to the public school which was the only schooling I had above sixth grade. I ended up leaving school the following April.

I remember the three-and-a-half mile walk to and from the Clonalton school as being quite frightening. We had to cross a paddock full of wild cows and goannas which were about six feet long and stood one foot off the ground. There was a particular goanna which menaced us—watching us with its beady eye and we ran screaming to the only tree in the paddock to escape it only to discover that it was heading for the same tree to escape us! The cows snorted and raked the ground with their hooves and that was frightening too. There were also plovers down from the house and they attacked us during breeding season so we ran like the wind holding our school cases over our heads to protect us as the birds just kept attacking us. That was the gauntlet we had to run to get to and from school for about four years.

After stints at other schools, I returned to Frogmore school four times. Each school I commenced in was learning something different. The schools I attended were small 'one teacher' schools with about fifteen students. Grade Six was the highest grade so I never had any difficulty settling back in.

Mr. Moylan

One of the teachers at Frogmore, Mr. Moylan, taught me to hate school. He was just the vilest creature. He'd sit up front looking down on fifteen kids or so, take his hanky out of his trouser pocket, snorkel back through his nose to clear out whatever was lurking there, and spit it out into his hanky. I'm talking about gollies. He was just a beast. I've never seen—or heard—anyone else do that. Blowing it out's one thing, but snorkling it back, making all those noises like he's drowning in his own snot...

The worst of it was his wife obviously cleaned and washed the filth out of his hankies. They were perfectly clean but he was just a pompous bastard and he treated the kids the same. He dressed immaculately. Always wore a tie. I reckon that was to cover up his Adam's apple as he was snorkelling, hide it while it bobbed up and down.

He wasn't a local man, he come from way beyond, I don't know where. He was sent to Frogmore. As far as I know they got rid of him out of teaching and put him in charge of a boy's home. They demoted him because he was cruel - bloody cruel. At that time in schools, the only thing teachers like Moylan understood was corporal punishment. It didn't worry me when he caned me because I was a mischievous little bugger. One time I called another kid a bastard and he went to the teacher boohooing and carrying on. The next day Moylan gave me six cuts with the feather duster. He had a feather duster with a cane handle and he used the cane part, not the feather part. It stung, let me tell you.

But the way he treated my sister Pauline was really unfair. Mum went to see him because we told her about him hitting Pauline. He would rap her across the knuckles with the edge of the ruler if she wasn't writing correctly or whatever. That's what I didn't like about schools back then. They were like concentration camps as far as I could see. In those days you used to write with a dip nib pen. Light upstrokes and heavy downstrokes. Beautiful writing. Dip it in the ink and away you'd go, getting the ink all over your fingers. Moylan picked on Pauline—I guess he picked on other kids too—but she was four years younger than me when she started school there. He was giving her whacks across the backs of her knuckles.

Pauline has arthritis in her hands these days and she blames Moylan for that. Although Mum had shocking arthritis too. Mum had the gold wires or rods drilled down through three of her toes on one foot and left in there for six weeks. They were sticking out the end of her toes, then they pulled them out with a pair of pliers. I think they did help a bit. Mum never went to school with Moylan so I can't blame him for that!

I've received a fifteen-inch wooden ruler with a metal strip running down one edge on the desk in front of me. I've had it for years. How I would have liked to cut Moylan across the bridge of his nose with the edge. That would hurt the most. I'd bring it down hard and say, 'There you go, you bastard.' He wouldn't be snorkelling for a while after that, let me tell you!

I had a natural ability for mathematics, but always missed the algebra part of the curriculum. I can do mental arithmetic quickly and effectively and managed to assist our daughter Diane with maths when she studied it at university. As for history and geography, I missed a great deal.

When I left school to go rabbiting, one of teachers made a written protest. His name was Jim Whale. He was a fantastic teacher in Boorowa. I got on well with him even though I spent a bit of time out in the hall. This was because I was always getting in trouble for laughing and cracking jokes. When I left school Mr Whale wrote a couple of letters to Mum and Dad begging them to send me back, because I had great potential and all this bullshit.

When I joined the New South Wales Police Force five years later I went to him and asked him to write me a reference. He said, 'I sure will.' He was pleased to because he had thought I was a lost cause out in the bush rabbiting, which is probably true. He wrote me a reference and I still have it today.

Sport

The thing I loved about school was the opportunity to play with other children. I missed out on that at the farm. We played active games every day including rounders, rugby league, tennis and cricket. With sport, the teacher simply chose two team captains and they had to pick their teams and everyone got to play. We had a tennis court at Uncle John's so Mum and I played tennis. Rugby League was a sport I played quite well and I continued to play until I joined the police at the age of nineteen. During my younger years I also did some boxing as did most boys at that time. We wore gloves but there were no real rules—just try to hurt your opponent as much as possible!

You might think I'd have a natural advantage at cricket and tennis, because we had a cricket pitch and a tennis court on the farm—but you'd be wrong. Tennis players would travel from town to town to play competition tennis, which bought them to Phill's Creek.

We spent a lot of time maintaining the court. Like many Australian bush tennis courts, it was made of ant bed. When we needed more gravel to top the court, we'd just go and rob an ants' nest! When you dug up an ants' nest you found this fine gravel, like hundreds and thousands made of clay. We used ant bed because it was easier to maintain than a lawn tennis court. If it was grass, you'd never keep the sheep from eating it! You'd fill any dents in the surface with this fine mix, drag bags over it to level the surface, then roll it with a concrete roller. The roller had an axle through the middle and you'd have to pull and pull on it to get it moving. If there were any ants left in the mix they'd be feeling pretty sorry for themselves by the time you'd run the roller over them.

Once you had a smooth surface you'd mix up some pipe clay to mark out the lines. But it didn't matter how many hours I spent preparing the court, or the number of times I went up and down with the roller. I was still a hopeless tennis player. My Mum loved tennis—she was a good player. I'd go down and have a hit with her and she's put it all over me. Sure, I could serve, but my backhand would just sail over the back or the side fence. I'm talking about up until when I was nineteen years old.

Some people have the hand-eye coordination you need, but I don't. If you threw a ball to me there'd be a good chance I wouldn't catch it. My hands will close up before it arrives, or after it's whizzed by!

I also hated cricket, much to Dad's disgust. He was a good cricketer and he always wanted me to play the game. We had a cricket pitch on the farm, so I couldn't avoid it. One time my Uncle John bought me a new cricket bat. We went off to play a match in Yass, the next town across from Boorowa. Bluey Shehans was on our team. He saw me arrive with a brand spanking new cricket bat, and asked if he can borrow it when he goes out to bat. 'All right,' I said, and he's off to the pitch. Two or three hits later the handle came out and my bat was stuffed. I'll never forgive Bluey for breaking my new bat! Even though I hated the game.

Now, let me tell you a bit about my early years of paid work. I tried my hand at a number of things, including making my contribution to reducing the rabbit plague which afflicted the country in the twentieth century.

CHAPTER SIX

Starting work

When I was about eleven years old, Dad won a contract to look after nine of the Pasture Protection Board's Travelling Stock Reserves. These reserves allowed drovers to feed their stock each night they were on the road. Sheep can only walk four miles a day, while cattle can manage eight. The reserves were fenced and maybe between thirty or forty acres. Dad went out and eradicated any rabbits, and cleared the noxious weeds.

During the school holidays I'd go and work with Dad for two or three weeks. We camped out in a tent, which I enjoyed. As Dad was working, there was no alcohol. I loved rabbiting; I didn't like digging out the burrs. We had to dig them out with a hoe. To the best of my knowledge they didn't use poison in those days. Dad had a team of fifteen dogs, and he knew them all by name. I remember the time I spent working with him as quite special—just working side by side and talking about our work, but never about anything more personal.

Dad didn't talk much. He wasn't much for reminiscing. You'd work all day from daylight until dusk, when the light faded and you couldn't see what you were doing. There was no such thing as an eight-hour workday back them. You'd get up early, and go around to check the traps before the crows could get to them. Come back to the camp, have brekky at sunup, then go and dig out rabbit burrows or burrs. After maybe three hours you'd come back to cook lunch. Dad had a camp oven, and he was a pretty good cook. He'd cook up a stew of meat, potato and pumpkin. The meat wouldn't keep long, so he'd sometimes have some sent out by mail, if there was a mail service nearby. Every now and then we'd eat rabbit, although I wasn't fond of them. Rabbit was too gamey for my liking.

Dad had a homemade cooler in his tucker box. It measured two and a half feet long, a foot high, and one and a half feet deep, with leather hinges and mesh on the ends. It's where he kept his butter and meat. We never had fresh milk—we used condensed milk if anything. We'd always return to the camp for smoko in the morning and afternoon, which kept the day buzzing along. Around dusk, Dad would cook a meal over the fire on a black firepan griddle. The meat he cooked that way ended up tasting better than a barbeque, I reckon.

I loved being out in the bush with Dad. I was only a kid, and didn't have any adult conversation, so there wasn't much to talk about. He'd say, 'Listen boy, we'd better go around and see to the traps.' He was a disciplinarian. I just did what he said.

He didn't treat me badly. I was company for him, someone for him to talk to, but I had nothing to say back. I was never game to contradict him. Don't ask questions, that was the unspoken rule. Mind you, I was a bit of a bugger. I'd go back to the campsite with some excuse, always the same excuse. He always left his small Morris ute parked beside the tent. He'd leave the keys in it. I'd start it up, and drive it backwards and forwards. That's how I learned to use the gears and clutch. Then I'd go back to work. I was twelve years old. Not wise in the ways of the world. We'd dig out and set our rabbit traps, then have dinner.

In that job, Dad made quite good money—he was paid a wage but also kept the money for his rabbit skins and meat and dead wool (the wool cut from sheep that died on the move). At the end of that job, he had made enough money to buy a Morris utility car, in an elegant cream colour. He went to Sydney to take delivery of it—I remember him arriving back at Fern Hill around midnight with some booze in himself and a dozen beers in the back of the car. For some reason, he christened the car 'Fanny'.

Dad later sold that utility to replace it as he had successfully tendered for a mail run down our road, twenty-five miles each way. The customary tender period for the run was four years, but Dad tendered for an eight-year contract as it had been a wet season and the roads were difficult to negotiate. He was lucky—there were no other tenderers and he was successful. He then bought a 1.5 ton Morris light commercial truck for the run because there were times when he was collecting a bale of wool! He did the mail run three days each week!

He had to collect the mail in town (and at the same time he would collect bread, and parcels and other goods to deliver with the mail) and drive out to do the run and there were occasions when the pub opened before he left town... My brother in law Ken, sister Pat and I rescued him a few times by completing the deliveries for Dad. I recall Mum and I searching for him one night and coming upon the truck on its roof but no sign of Dad. Luckily, he had been found and taken to hospital but there was no modern communication to let the family know.

He ran the mail through his drunken stupor, then sold it after four years as a going concern. He made good money from the sale, and went for a holiday to Sydney with Mum and one of my sisters. He came back with a flying suit and gloves for me to wear on the motor bike.

Earlier, I mentioned Joe Herbert, who married my grandmother after my father was born. Herbert was a pig of a man but I got on all right with him. He was the biggest builder around town, and owned several farms. His shed's still there in Boorowa, with *J P Herbert* written across the side. He was a good carpenter who built big flash houses. He bought a sheep property eight miles from our farm. He was having trouble with his sheep dog, so he asked me to stay for a week to help with the mustering and drenching. I reckon that was just a ploy to get me down there with the horse. I loved riding horses. I rode down there and Joe and I got on really well. He was a good cook. But my sisters hated him—they reckoned he was a bloody creep. One of my sisters said he made some passes at her. I thought you had the right to say *no*, you said *no*, so let it be.

Although I never saw Joe and Dad together much, they seemed to get on all right. They never mixed in same circles. Joe would leave my grandmother at home while he went off playing cards in different houses around Boorowa. The places he went to play cards—let's just say I always suspected there might have been more to it than just cards. A couple of the women involved had fairly colourful reputations. The people who went to the card nights were upper class folk: the doctor, the solicitor, and big time business owners. Joe fitted in well with them.

He'd stay out until 3.00 or 4.00 AM, then come home. I never saw him coming home. I'd go and stay with my grandmother when Joe was away working somewhere, but I didn't like to stay when he was there. He was a big strong sour bloke who didn't stand any nonsense. The only time he and I got on well together was when I mustered his rotten sheep.

Me at 14 years old & sister Pat at 16.

Although I had been in paid work beforehand, I left school permanently at fourteen, despite the written protest of one of my teachers. I began working as a professional rabbiter.

I had been making snares to catch rabbits since I was six years old. I was limited to snares at that age as traps were too dangerous—my sister Joan caught her hand in a trap when she was five. Pat told me about it; I didn't see it happen. Fortunately Joan recovered with no permanent damage, but they *were* dangerous.

You didn't let little kids near rabbit traps, they're mongrels of things. They're so sensitive they go off at the touch of a hat. When you're setting one you flip the little keeper over, and hold the tongue up from underneath the jaws. You need enough strength to squeeze the trap with your right hand and set the tongue with your left. All the time praying it doesn't go off! You want to get your fingers out from underneath as quickly as you can. I've been caught few times when my thumb slipped. If they catch you on your thumbnail it turns black and falls out.

Once you've set the trap you'd place it in the ground, and put a piece of paper over the tongue. That's so when you sprinkle some dirt over it you don't block the mechanism, and stop it from going off. We'd tear up these little pieces of paper and have them pinned to our shirt. If you were too close when you were sprinkling the dirt and the thing went off, it'd bloody get you.

So when I was a kid we placed snares, which were nooses made from wire, into which the rabbit placed its head and as it ran the snare tightened and strangled it.

In the 1940s rabbits were in plague proportions—you could see the farmland just writhing with them. They were the sworn enemy of the farmer and so from a young age we were actively engaged in eradicating the rabbits. We knew the spots to place the snares and were also experienced at burning them out with fire in winter to chase them out of the felled logs. We helped the adults poison them using strychnine baits mixed in with chopped thistle root. Strychnine death is hideous but we picked up around 100 carcasses each morning, pegged them out to dry and sold the skin stacks to the skin buyers. We also shot them which was much more for fun.

When I turned professional, I used traps and set about seventy each night. The traps were placed near their warrens or where there were fresh droppings in the afternoon and then I patrolled around ten pm. In that round I cleared and reset the traps. The next patrol was sunrise when traps were cleared and reset. It was important to get out before the crows and blowflies got to them. Every third day you needed to alter the location of the traps—rabbits are cunning. It never ceased to amaze me that twenty-four pairs had arrived with the first fleet and so quickly bred into a massive population needing dramatic culling.

In addition to the trapping, I resorted often to digging, which was demanding work. Digging required you to dig the burrows out, by hand, relying on your dogs to hunt the rabbits. At various times, I had a pack of up to fifteen dogs, many of them beagles.

When I was trapping, usually the trapped rabbit was still alive, one leg in the trap, squealing in pain and fright. I was efficient in wringing their necks and ending their misery. Then you put the carcass in a large hessian bag which sat across the rump of the horse behind the saddle. The other option for carrying them was to cut through the lower part of the leg, fold the other leg through the cut you had made, and hook the carcass over a hook hanging from the side of the saddle. All the rabbits were brought back home—they were not gutted in the paddocks because that attracted the crows.

After we gutted them we buried the offal. The skinned rabbits were then hung out in the hessian bags on the nearest main road and the man from the freezing works collected them and sold the meat, leaving the money raised on his next trip past. In those times, we all relied on an honour system and no one locked their homes even though it was widely known that people held cash stacked in trunks under their beds, particularly when wool prices were good.

As winter approached, the skins became more valuable and so we skinned the rabbits, pegged the skins out to dry and sold the skins. The meat was sometimes boiled up, mixed with wheat and fed to the dogs or any pig we might be fattening. Before I left school, I used the money I earned from rabbiting to buy shoes and clothes, as did my sister Pat. In those days, to extend the life of the shoes, we applied half-soles or stuffed the shoes with cardboard so your feet did not touch the gravel through the holes in your shoes.

My first full time job, working on Mr. Cooper's farm—the same Mr. Cooper who had argued with Uncle John—earned me four pounds each week. In those days, the standing arrangement was that the trapper kept and was able to sell the skins because you were helping the farmer clear the land of rabbits. However, I had the misfortune of working for one of the meanest men in our community. Mr. Cooper demanded that he receive one half of my skins.

My rabbiting career came to a halt suddenly in about 1950, when I was around fifteen. The viral disease myxomatosis was introduced and was wildly successful in decimating the rabbit population and there was no work for rabbiters. I missed that work because it was a way of life I loved.

CHAPTER SEVEN

Dad

By the end of his life my father was an utter bum around town, a hopeless alcoholic. A down and out. It was sad to see that side of him. He spent his last couple of months in hospital, on and off. Then he went in for a couple of weeks and never came out. He died of a coronary, which means he had a clot in the blood stream. When it moves far enough it wipes you out. That's what I understand.

When Dad died it was one of the largest funerals ever seen in Boorowa. There was a Catholic priest who died—I can't remember his name—who drew a bigger crowd, but Dad's was still one of the best attended funerals in the town.

There were plenty of reasons why people liked him. He was a hard worker, and he always carried plenty of cash to hand out to all the bums who'd hang around him at the pub. Never mind that he was stingy with us. If Mum asked him for ten quid he'd refuse, but he'd splash it around at the pub, no problems. He'd lend ten quid to any barfly that asked, and never expect to see it again.

Mind you, one time a boss refused to pay my wages, Dad went in to front him. So he'd stand up for his family when it was necessary.

From an outsider's point of view he was a great bloke who got on well with everyone. Some of my stories make him sound like a mongrel, but he really wasn't. He worked hard, and I learned a lot from him. Sometimes his ideas paid off, sometimes they didn't. Here are some other stories that show more of his personality and character.

Getting bogged

Dad would get in a car and never think twice before driving it across the ground after it had been raining. Getting bogged was a major thing. We're talking about driving off the road, pretty much anywhere. The tracks he used were meant for horse carts, but he'd drive over them. As a result, he was an expert at getting cars out once he got bogged.

He always reacted calmly when he found himself in strife. I never heard Dad swear. None of us kids ever heard him swear. He gave me the biggest flogging ever when he heard me swearing once. I'd say he was philosophical and patient. Nothing seemed to bother him. You'd hear the rear wheels spinning in the mud, like the ground was rotten. He'd say, 'Looks like a bit of a hiccup here.' Nothing seemed to trouble him.

Then it'd be all the kids out of the car, all hands on deck. Quite often I was the only kid with him. He'd say 'We've got to cord it, boy.' He always called me boy, which I didn't like.

Cording was his way of getting unstuck. There was always plenty of timber around, so he'd cut some poles, and use one to lift the car enough to slip some cording pieces of timber under the back wheels, to get some traction. Back in those days the cars were light, like our Model A Ford. So with a decent length of pole you could lift it up enough to get the job done. I'd get down and dirty, with mud all over my hands and knees, and poke as many logs as possible under the wheels. Then he'd let the car down on those pieces of timber.

Mind you, it might take two days to get a car out of a bog. I'm not joking about that.

We always seemed to get bogged within walking distance—three or four miles was considered walking distance—of our camp, or the farm at Fern Hill. I used to go rabbiting with him when he had a contract. Around Fern Hill when things got wet these bottomless bog holes appeared, so there were plenty of opportunities to get bogged. After Dad had let the car back down, he'd build a road of logs to get clear of the boggy section.

When we were building a house at Molong we struck one of these bog holes. We had to get the council to come in, dig it out and fill it with gravel. The hole was deeper than the D8 dozer. It wasn't like quicksand. More a whole lot of clay that turns into a spew hole—that's what we called them. If you jumped on a point you'd see the water oozing up three feet away. There was no base to it, unless you went down far enough.

These skills of Dad's came in handy after he got the mail run I mentioned earlier. When he was on the mail run he had a couple of wet seasons, including the first season after he bought it. He'd fixed up a lot of the road for the council with his cording system. If you drove over it at any speed it was like driving over a cattle grid. He used slats of round timber to spread the weight.

No way would I have been as calm as him if I got bogged. I would have gone off my block! Many years later when our kids were young, my wife and I took them up to Fern Hill. We went for a drive up to what used to be the orchard, up the back of the shearing shed, to see if any trees were still alive. Like an idiot, I drove into this little gully, covered with beautiful green grass. How deceptive it can be. We came to a grinding halt in the mud. I walked down to the woolshed and found a pile of old timber slabs. So I carried them up to try to do what Dad had done. Turns out I never learned a thing off him! My attempt to salvage the car was a complete failure!

Luckily Cliff, the bloke we'd leased the property to, came over on his tractor to say g'day. 'What the bloody hell you doing there?' he said.

'What's it look like I'm bloody doing, Cliff?' I said. 'I'm bogged to the axles.'

He told me to hang on a sec. He went off and came back with a wire rope with a hook on it. Hooked it onto his tractor and pulled us out.

That's how soft the ground can be. The water table was right up near the surface, but you couldn't see it. I should have known better after travelling around with Dad.

Me at 16 years old at Fern Hill before it all rotted.

Me 50 + years later at old at Fern Hill after it all rotted.

Mind you, the ground at Fern Hill was rock hard in the dry. I had to dig the long drop toilet holes. I've dug two in my life. You'd drive the crow bar in and go down maybe three-quarters of an inch—if you were lucky. Then when it was wet the ground just fell in on itself. But Cliff hauled us out of the bog and we went home happy as Larry.

Crayfishing at the dam

Dad was expert at crayfishing—we called them yabbies. He carried a pushbike rim with hessian tied all around it. He'd tie some bits of meat inside the bike rim, and throw it in the dam. The poor silly crayfish would get hold of the meat and he'd haul it in. He used binding twin as a rope—it was easy to carry a roll. Then he'd put the crayfish in salty water, to purge them. We'd fry them up and eat them. Delicious.

Duck shooting with 12 gauge

Dad took every opportunity to live off the land. When there were ducks about he'd creep up to the edge of the dam, and with a bit of luck or not—depending on which way it went—he'd bring down a duck. Mind you, you'd end up with more pellets than duck meat. There are seven shots in a 12 gauge, and that's a lot of pellets. I wasn't allowed to touch his shotgun. I was nineteen before he allowed me to use the 12 gauge.

I had a pea shooter rifle all my life. I only got rid of it when Howard brought in the gun laws after Port Arthur. I still reckon everyone should be allowed to have a gun. There shouldn't be any question about my right to own a gun. If I'd applied for one I probably would have been OK, but I wasn't going to put myself through all that. So I gave my .22 to a bloke who had a farm up in Wellington. NSW. It's still up there. I had no real use for it. I wasn't going to shoot anything. It was just one of those things I kept it in the cupboard. I could never hit a duck with a .22. I tried many times and missed every time. I had a bit more luck with the 12 gauge. By the time I'd stick my head over the bank, they'd be gone! Ducks are very alert.

When you started to eat the duck you'd wonder why you bothered shooting them. Wild ducks were rotten things to eat. It was like eating rabbit—they had this gamey taste. Dad would down a duck, cut it up and fry it. No wonder they were so tough. He should have boiled them but he didn't have the water. When we went camping he'd take a couple of four gallon drums of water. By the time you take a bit to wash and cook and make four pots of tea each day, it doesn't take long to use up all the water.

There was no fresh water to be found out where we were. The creeks usually had a dead sheep in them somewhere upstream. There's been times when I've been so thirsty I've laid on my belly and drunk from the creek, but I always think afterwards—oh Jesus! That poor dead sheep. When they get weak they get stuck in the water and cark it.

There were no purification tablets in those days. You relied on your gut to do all that for you...

Bottles for jam

Dad provided Mum with plenty of bottles for jam. He made them out of empty beer bottles—long-neck bottles, no stubbies in those days. He'd make a ring out of a piece of wire, clip a handle to it, and put it in the fire until it glowed red hot. Then he'd place it over the neck of the bottle, down to the shoulder where he'd sized it to fit. Then he's dip the bottle in a bucket of water and kapow! You've got a bottle for jam.

There might have been some sharp edges but you didn't worry about that. With Dad there were no shortage of bottles! When Mum made the jam she'd pour some wax over the top once it had cooled down, then paste two or three layers of paper over the top. She made the paste from flour and water.

Mum made bucketloads of jam. She used whatever ingredients were plentiful—lemon, plums, melons. We used to grow pine melons down by the creek, so we'd have gallons of melon and lemon jam. She also used to make a lot of plum jam. I really got to hate that plum jam.

It was too much of the same thing, over and over. 'What jam are we having tonight?' 'Melon and lemon.' 'What jam are we having tonight?' 'Melon and lemon.' It just went on and on. I like the bread but not the jam. The girls liked it, but I didn't. I'm a bit of a fussy eater.

Gardening down by Phill's Creek

Dad's market garden came and went with the seasons. He always had a garden down by Phill's Creek. Up on the banks was a bit of fenced-off land, with a hand pump for pumping the water out of the creek to water the garden. He's put up wire netting to keep rabbits out. He'd grow pumpkins, spinach, radish and rhubarb. The rhubarb was beautiful, a prolific grower with big red stalks. I've got seven plants growing down beside the house here. We don't eat it anymore because we're bloody sick of it, but everyone comments on how beautiful it is. Dad grew them in a four gallon tin with the bottom cut out. The tin protected it from the snails.

I did the same here before I got it established. I bought some black pots from the nursery and cut the bottoms out.

There were another ten acres down by the creek where Dad grew peas one year. He put in three or four rows, and when they were ready we picked them and bagged then up in chaff bags. The chaff bags were the next size up from wheat bags. They were made from the kind of coarse hessian you'd use to make a Coolgardie safe. You could pack one hundred pounds of peas into them.

We all helped with the pea picking—Jeez, that's hard on your back. Then we took the bags to the railway station at Boorowa, and put them on the train to Sydney. The money we got back was exactly what it cost to freight them to Sydney. So the whole exercise was worth nothing!

Dad never grew peas again.

Next he grew potatoes in the 10 acre paddock for a couple of years. I drove the two horses to sow the potatoes—I still have the plough here in the back yard. It's a two furrow plough, and I felt like the captain of the ship when I drove it. Uncle John dropped the potatoes in. When other farmers were growing spuds they'd use a tractor. One of them would sit up on the back of the plough and drop the spuds off as they were pulled along by a tractor. Not us—we had two horses. For a couple of years we got fantastic crops of potatoes. I've got photos of us digging up the potatoes.

Growing and digging the potatoes was easy. Selling them was tricky. They had the Potato Board in those days. You had to sell through the Board, which charged a commission. As you might imagine, that wasn't Dad's style. He sold a lot of potatoes around the place. He got in with the hotels and cafes in town, and they bought potatoes off him. They loved his potatoes. This went on for weeks until someone dobbed him in to the Potato Board. He was caught selling potatoes without a licence, and had to cop a fine. It seems ridiculous that you needed a licence to sell potatoes. Back then, it was the same with wheat and everything. I suppose there's reasons for it, to stop people flooding the market, but it never made sense to me.

Dad also found himself in trouble with the Wheat board one time. Someone had been selling wheat in his name. Dad never grew wheat. The Board got onto him for it, but he didn't do it.

So the potatoes didn't work out. Then Dad and Uncle Teddy decided to go into big time gardening up behind the house, in the same gully where I got bogged years later and Cliff had to tow me out. Those two idiots started digging a well. They managed six feet before it got too hard. Dad had bought a brand spanking new Howard rotary hoe, the sort you walk behind, and they'd started fencing the block to grow spinach. They would have been smarter to dig the well before they spent their money. It was another brainwave of Dad's that didn't pay off.

As a result, we had nothing. We were living on potatoes, like the Irish. Teddy and his wife were staying with us. He'd get up

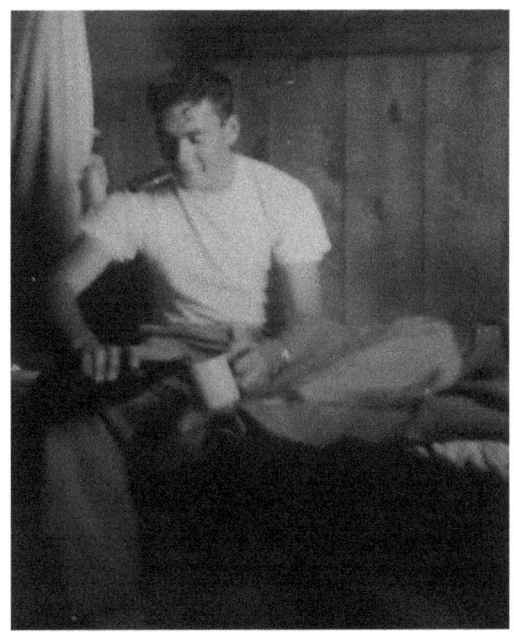

Me at 16 years old.

and cook up a batch of potatoes for breakfast. You've got to be joking, haven't you?

Dad's truck.

Shearing

Dad was a good shearer. He wasn't the fastest, but he was certainly the cleanest. Watching him shear was beautiful. He'd just glide along, shearing 120 to 130 sheep a day. He didn't make any second cuts or leave any dags. The fast shearers go like hell. They'd do 220 or 230 sheep in the same time.

Shearing 100 sheep a day meant shearing one every five minutes. The shearing sheds ran on a strict timeframe. The bell rang, and off you'd go. After two hours they'd ring the bell for smoko. If you caught a sheep on the bell, you had five minutes finish the job. After smoko, there'd be another two hours to lunch, then two hours until afternoon smoko, and two hours until you knocked off. You couldn't catch a sheep after the bell had rung for lunch or smoko. Those were the union rules.

The fast clean shearers are the best. They make a lot of money Our best man's son won the World Shearing Championships in USA once. He wasn't the fastest, but he was fast and clean enough to win. Dad was sought after because he was clean. He didn't treat the sheep rough. A lot of shearers belt the sheep into submission with the handpiece—they're hard those handpieces.

I found out later that Dad was the ringer at the shed down the road, so he must have sped up. As a labourer, he was always a union man for sure.

Myself, I really got to hate these union bastards the first time I went shearing. I'd cadged enough money off my parents to buy the petrol needed to drive up to Queensland. I was only seventeen, and I didn't have any money left. So I lined up all ready to start outside the shed, when this standover bloke come up to me and demanded to see my union ticket.

I said, 'I haven't got one.'

He said, 'You've got to have one before you can start.'

'You bastard,' I thought. I told him I didn't know this before I came out here, and I didn't have any money. He softened up a little, and they could take the fee out of my first lot of pay. It might have only been four or five quid, but it killed me at the time. That's how it was, they stood over you. I don't like standover tactics. Absolute shockers, the lot of them.

Having said, that for the twelve years I worked in the Fire Brigade I was in the Union. They weren't standover people. If anything, we stood over them! Management tried to bring in this stupid law that all firemen had to have an overcoat.

We got a group together by phone. All the fire stations were connected by phone, so we rang around and checked if people were in favour of this bullshit. Sydney's a mild climate, you wouldn't wear an overcoat in a fit. We all got together and decided to go in and put the kybosh on it. And we did. That's my experience with unions.

Anyway, I spent a season shearing in Queensland, then came down and stayed with my Uncle and Aunt in Wellington. I joined he police force in April when I was 19.

A decent bloke

There was a fair bit of goodness in Dad. He dedicated himself to what he was doing. He could go weeks out in the bush without drinking, but as soon as he got the smell of a cork the poor bastard was gone.

He was not a hopeless alcoholic when we were kids, but become one later. I remember seeing him sitting in the gutter in Boorowa when we were visiting. I just wouldn't go anywhere near him. That was very sad.

The grog was all he had left. He was living with a couple of other drunks too.

I don't know if he was disappointed with himself. He never apologised to anyone, never commented on anything. He just did what he did. If he felt any remorse within himself he never showed it to us. Maybe he didn't remember, because his brain was fogged out. He knew how to do the right thing. In the beginning, he wasn't going to come to my wedding. In the end he came, because I gave him an ultimatum. He didn't come to Diane's christening. It annoyed him that our kids were bought up in the Methodist church, and he found it hard to put his prejudices aside when it really mattered.

The Frogmore Farmer

How I wish I'd had longer conversations with him! I regret it now, but I couldn't bring myself to talk to him about his drinking. How do you approach it? 'You're an alcoholic, can we do something about it?' I didn't have a clue what to do. I have terrible remorse over that at times. I'd take one lousy bottle of beer over when we visited him and that would just set him off, wanting more. We'd take him food, spend the afternoon, and leave him with a solitary bottle of beer. Just enough to awaken his thirst. He was thirteen-and-a-half miles from town, and with no transport. That was the wrong thing to do.

My father at 55 years old.

CHAPTER EIGHT

More work

I can honestly say that I have been a hard worker all my life, and have always applied myself to the best of my ability to the job at hand.

My first 'off-farm' income started when I was twelve. My sisters were to go to boarding school and there was a nearby family with a boy, Gregory, about to start school. As a three-mile walk was required, his parents asked me to live with them, rent free, and walk him to and from school each day in exchange for being paid one pound each week. The family were in our church and were family friends. I came to see for the first time a different, more prosperous, way of living. Their farm was much larger than ours, there was a much greater variety of food and life was comfortable.

Later, when I was about sixteen years old, I worked as a farmhand at a local property for a childless couple and lived with them. They had just built a new home—I enjoyed a room of my own with beautiful rosewood furniture. Having slept on a veranda at home, I became increasingly aware that there was a better life for some people than the one I had as a child.

When I was fourteen years old, I started work at a pest control firm in Sydney. Mum organised the job for me with a relative of hers. It was in that job I had my first lessons in building construction. I was assisting a carpenter to repair and rebuild after vermin and white ants damaged property, and I recall working on lots of parquetry floors.

The problem wasn't the job, but the accommodation. One of Mum's uncles arranged for me to stay at the Salvos, which was just horrible. My ceiling was made out of wire mesh; it was like living in a cage. Every time I strummed my guitar someone would be shouting at me to shove it up my arse. I never saw hardly any of the people who lived there. They all came and left in their own time, or slept through the day. It was a bunch of no-hopers in the centre of Sydney. A slum. It smelled awful. The absolute pits. About three months later, I was so homesick that I left that job to return home. I thought Sydney and I would never get on again.

I had expected better of the Salvos because when Uncle John and I would travel down to Sydney we'd stay at the People's Palace in Pitt Street. It wasn't an expensive place but the dining room had beautiful white tablecloths, white serviettes, and silver napkin rings. When Uncle John and I had a meal, I felt like a bloody king. I hadn't realised that the Salvos also provided lodgings for derelicts.

After I returned to Boorowa I worked with Jack Quinn, a carpenter at the tungsten mine at Frogmore. It was an old wolfram or scheelite dig that had been abandoned ten, fifteen, maybe even twenty years ago. I saw the mine from its commencement until it closed. I had various different roles there. Initially, we lived on site in two-man tents, with a bush toilet—a shovel under a tree! Jack taught me everything he knew about building which stood me in good stead for the future. We built huts for the single men (the engineer, the manager and the winch operator) and we built a mess hall. He and I built three-roomed huts. They were an oblong building with a partition down the middle which created three rooms, a door opening to the outside and there was room for two single beds in there. They were lined with a sugar cane by-product, canite and had an asbestos roof and exterior walls. The windows were Cooper louvre windows.

Sketch of the Frogmore mine.

I had a ton of energy in those days and my great passion was playing football—I looked forward to finishing work each day so I could get down to football training which involved passing a ball down by the river.

My work there also included making poppet heads to get the miners down the mine shaft. The poppet head stands above the shaft and is also used to winch out the ore. When the shaft was first sunk, the miners worked out laterally, chasing the tungsten ore. They'd go down twenty-five feet and put in a ladder, build a little platform, then go down another twenty-five feet. The ladders were made from two-by-four Oregon stringers with 3/8 inch steel rods as rungs.

When the mine was abandoned they left the ladders in the shaft.

Of course, during the years when the mine was closed the shaft slowly filled with water. Our team had to go down and repair the ladders and landings. We had a water pump going to draw the water out. Keith Bolding, supposedly my second-best mate after Jack, was the first man to go down into the mine. A right liar, was Keith. He had his big chest puffed out and he stepped onto the ladder, but the platform twenty-five feet down was rotten from being underwater so long. The whole thing collapsed, taking Keith down with it. He ended up in the water, with his feet and legs tangled in the rungs of the ladder.

Up top the cry goes up, 'Man down!' Everyone flies into a panic, the boss is running around like the proverbial rooster with its head chopped off. Keith had taken in a gobful of water, so he wasn't saying much. Someone had the presence of mind to grab a rope and throw it down to Keith. There was no other way to reach him. Luckily he wasn't knocked out by the fall, or that would have been the death of him. In the end he grabbed hold of the rope and we hauled him up to safety.

As the mine progressed I helped set up the ore processing plant consisting of two sets of jaws, roller conveyor belts, two jig tables which move backwards, forwards and sideways while the water washes over it and the heavy ores—scheelite and wolframite—fall to the bottom. I was not a miner but worked around the mine on the equipment and buildings. I was learning all the time about carpentry and mechanical engineering.

The mine processor worked around the clock and at one stage my father got a job working on the night shift with me although he never lived on site—he travelled from the farm and back each day. So I saw the mine from beginning to end—working with the carpenter to build buildings and the engineer to build mine equipment. In the summer I carted wheat during the day and then worked the night shift at the mine. I got strong quickly, lifting wheat in 180 pound bags. The first time I was completely unprepared for the weight of a bag and it dropped me to the floor. The bag came off a bag loader which lifted the bag and I had to get the bag off the loader, and my first time I ended up flat on my back on the back of the semi-trailer! I was certainly embarrassed but learned quickly how to put my shoulder into it to take the weight and I successfully caught the next bag. In fact, that was a good lesson to learn and resulted in me having shoulder surgery later in my life from the load my shoulders took in my various lines of work.

The boss on that job failed to pay me one week and Dad went in to the pub and demanded my pay until he paid. That was one time I was grateful for Dad's intervention.

At the mine when I was nearly seventeen I was promoted and so was in charge of the brand-new truck and a brand-new Ford utility. My duties included

Me at 16 years old with a bunch of "mine" guys acting the goat.

driving the miner's children to school, transporting the ore to Sydney and, each Saturday, taking mine folk to Boorowa for supplies and for any social activities—they climbed into the back of the truck and I drove them to town and back.

I only worked at that mine for two-and-a-half years before it closed again. The whole business was dodgy from the start. There are some shonks around. What happened in this case is they decided to reopen an old mine and list it on the stock market. They'd find a lode of scheelite and hype up the quality of the ore. Up go the shares, they cash out, then they say oops, the lode's not as good as we thought. Or maybe the price of tungsten goes down. The scheelite's probably still there but it's not economical to work it.

During that time, my Uncle Kevin was shearing and after the mine had closed I spent some time as a roustabout in the shearing sheds with him. My work was to do the bidding of everyone in the shed—picking up the wool in the shed and other general work. We travelled from shed to shed around Ivanhoe, Dirranbandi and those areas. Uncle Kevin was a top shearer and was sought after so we had plenty of work.

Kevin had a 2 ½ ton truck he used when he went shearing. It had a frame around the tray about three feet high. If he got caught in bad weather he'd throw a tarp over the frame and camp in the truck. He worked everywhere from Goulburn up to Mungindi on the Moree Plains, through to Dirranbandi and St George in southern Queensland. Many a time that tarp kept him dry. I was travelling with him and another shearer one time when Kevin arranged to pick up a third shearer from the hospital in town. The shearer had been injured, but he'd been patched up. Kevin spoke with the boss and offered to bring the bloke back to the shed.

That was all good, except the other shearer went and got on the booze, and started creating a nuisance with the nurses. This was just a little country hospital, no security guards or anything like that. Kevin marched in, grabbed the bloke by the scruff of the neck, and wheeled him outside. Remember, Kevin's not a big man, but he was very solidly built. Of course, the drunken shearer took a swing at him, so Kevin let him have one right in the guts. Then he picked him up bodily and threw him over the frame into the back of the truck.

Me and Kevin and the bloke he'd taken out of the hospital sat in the cab as we headed back to the shed, with the drunk lying in the back on the tray. Never heard a peep out of him until we arrived at the shed fifty miles down the road.

Another time Kevin and I were out on a property together. The shearers slept two to a room, so Kevin and I bunked in together. I wasn't a shearer—I was just a young fella, a rouseabout. The bloke in the next room kept aggravating Kevin. You know, talking rubbish, making stupid noises, trying to provoke him. It was a Sunday, and Kevin was patching his trousers. Shearing trousers, Mum always called them. When they wore out Kevin would sew canvas onto them to make them last longer.

So he's sewing and sewing and sewing, and he and I are chatting away, and the bloke in the next room's letting his mouth run away with him. I'm watching Kevin's hand. It starts to shake, and then he's missing a stitch here, a stitch there with that bloody great needle. This bloke's still rabbiting on and eventually Kevin stands up, goes to his door, and tells him to shut up. The bloke tells him to get stuffed, in so many words. Kevin storms into his room, lifts up the bed with the bloke on it, and turns it upside down on top of him. Well, that had the desired effect. Didn't hear a word from him after that.

I admired him for that. He'd defend himself if someone was doing the wrong thing. Not many people would have the guts. But once you wound Kevin up—bam, bam, bam, and you'd be down for the count. He was fiery, all right. When he was a young bloke he used to train with a boxer who lived in Newcastle. Not Les Darcy, but a bloke like Les Darcy, well-known. After that Kevin fancied himself as a bit of a pug. Not that I'm one to criticise—I found those two episodes most entertaining!

I found shearing to be back-breaking work, even though there was some mechanisation with petrol motors driving the shearer's handpieces. My back just ached and I attribute my current back problems to that work. I could shear around 140 sheep in one day, others could shear 200 in a day. When a shearer cut a sheep, which happened easily and often because of the pace you had to work at, it was the shearer's responsibility to stitch any wounds. Once we finished stitching, we yelled 'Tar!' and the tar boy would come running with the bucket of tar for us to daub on and around the wound to keep the blow flies off the wound.

Sheep can be difficult to manage—they can give a strong kick and the shearer is in a vulnerable position, bending over the sheep. To shear a sheep you take the belly wool off first, then go up the neck and take off the top notch then shear the outside back leg and then 'the long blow' from the tail to the top of the neck. A novice shearer can get distracted by a kicking sheep and let go of the beast and they will take off! The sheep bolts with the shorn fleece dragging around behind on the shed floor and it can look pretty amusing, although not to the boss who wanted the fleece kept clean, not dragged around in the dirt!

I recall being in a shed with Uncle Don, one of Mum's three

brothers who were shearers. I was in the shed working and the radio was on in the shed. An announcement came over the air: 'A special announcement—Happy Birthday to X and we have a special request to play for you.' We all knew that X was in a relationship with a local aboriginal woman and the song they played, right through, was 'On Top of Old Smokey'! They were pretty rough at times.

Initially, we travelled in a caravan with an annex, in which I slept, because Uncle Kevin's wife Aunt Irene was with us. She was expecting a child and as her time drew nearer Uncle Kevin took her and the van back to Goulburn and he and I continued travelling in the truck. After I had shorn for some months, I was afflicted with the shearer's curse known as yolk boils, a painful condition arising from human contact with sheep with a bacterial infection. When Uncle Kevin had them, he was unable to drive the truck so I did the driving

My sisters excited about my new bike.

while he slept. I had learned how to drive from studying Dad at the wheel and then practicing in my head depressing the clutch, changing through the gears. There was a bad moment one day when I hit the brakes very hard to avoid a herd of kangaroos which suddenly appeared in the middle of the road—unfortunately they were a figment of my imagination. Uncle Kevin woke up with a rude shock when his head hit the dashboard! Fortunately, he was a tough man and was unaffected by the blow to his head, although he did insist on taking back the driving!

I became interested in motorbikes at about the age of fifteen, when I bought my first Bantam, which enabled me to speed around the farm. Uncle Kevin and I both had motor bikes which travelled with us. Over the years I owned a variety of bikes and I enjoyed tinkering with them and riding—ultimately I had a Triumph Thunderbird 650 which was the same bike as the police force used, very powerful.

Modern photo of a Triumph Thunderbird 650.

The Frogmore Farmer

The road into town was gravel. If Kevin and I were riding our motor bikes into town and were stuck behind a slow car, we placed ourselves on each side of the car and overtook it at the highest speed our bikes could do, spewing up gravel into their path in the process. Of course, in those days there were no helmets—just hop on and go like the proverbial. I loved racing along corrugated dirt roads—once I saw my speed was 90 miles per hour!

It is funny to look back at the things I did when I was younger and some of the devilment I got into—how foolhardy I was, in a way. I am also mindful that I was lucky I caused no serious harm.

I still remember feeling like a real rebel when two mates and I unscrewed the exhausts from our bikes and sped through town with our bikes roaring! We hid in the bush, well concealed, awaiting the long arm of the law which was in hot pursuit! The local police officer was Jack Sparkes and his trusty steed was, at least until he was provided with a car, a police horse. We watched him ride past us and then back towards town, and after our bikes had cooled down screwed the exhausts back on and rode home when he was out of sight and earshot. What we were forgetting was that we were the only motor bike owners in the entire town so sophisticated detective skills were not required to identify the wrongdoers... Luckily for us he was a family friend and a thoroughly decent man and he was the inspiration for me to want to join the police.

There was also the famous incident of The Cake. Weekend dances were an important aspect of our social life. The appeal for us as young men, apart from the girls, was the supper which doubled for us as our evening meal.

As we had to pay to enter, our habit was to enquire as to

whether supper had been served already. If it had, we left and headed to another dance. We could travel anywhere between ten and forty miles for a dance! This particular night, we travelled to Rye Park, asked if supper had been served and, when told it had not been, paid our entry fee and went in—only to find supper was finished! In a prominent position on the stage was The Cake, which had won first prize at the show that day. Some bright spark decided we should take The Cake and eat it outside for our supper. The Cake was picked up on the run and passed between us like a football as we exited from the hall, closely followed by the local policeman who managed to grab a couple of my co-conspirators but continued chasing us outside as we scattered in all directions. I heard him shout 'Halt or I'll fire" which made me run faster—straight into a wire fence which ricocheted me backwards and I landed flat on my back. I was up again and running like the wind within seconds, got through the fence and then discovered my legs were pounding away in thin air—then I dropped like a stone into a dry creek bed. None of us got a morsel of that cake, but I was free.

My friends, stopped by the police, were arrested and locked up for the night. A couple of days later, overcome with Catholic guilt, I went to Sergeant Story's home at Boorowa to confess my part in the heinous crime; he told me to go away. Later, after the others had been convicted and fined, one of their

Fern Hill before veranda and bathroom was added.

fathers came to Dad and demanded that he contribute one half of the fine. Dad left them in no doubt that he had no intention of making a contribution.

When a Peugeot 203 won the Redex trial in 1953, I bought myself one. It had a soft top and was great fun to drive. I did draw the line, though, when an acquaintance climbed into my Peugeot carrying his twelve gauge shotgun with him, instructing me to take him into the nearby town of Young. He promptly positioned himself standing on the front seat, with the roof down firing off and blowing the letterboxes we passed to smithereens!

I did my own mechanical work on the Peugeot, greasing and oiling, cleaning the motor and polishing the tyres. There was a time the car had a brake failure—I simply pulled the wheel and brake drum off at the roadside, although a few parts fell off. I put it all back together again as best I could, but put the loose parts in the boot for Dad to fix it later. Six months on, I had a problem with the distributor and adopted the same approach. I dismantled it and reassembled it at the roadside as best I could, putting aside the weights from the distributor for a proper repair later— 'later' never came, the repairs were never completed but the car was driving perfectly well, with the spare parts in the boot!

I once had a passenger refuse to travel any further with me in that car when I sped up the very steep spillway and raced around it at Wyangala Dam to show the amazing capacity of my car in challenging terrain. He screamed at me to stop and let him out, which I did, and he refused to return to the car.

On rare occasions I borrowed Uncle John's MG TD. I had an agreement with Uncle John to keep the MG TD serviced when I was using it. Jack accompanied me to Sydney on one trip and I left the car at Liverpool for a service. While they had it, they damaged the front grill. Jack and I came back to Uncle Don at Crookwell, told him of the problem and he said 'No worries—I'll fix it with some red paint and no one will ever know'. He did the job and Uncle John, to the best of my knowledge, never found out.

The Peugeot also got a thrashing on my numerous trips between Fern Hill and Grabben Gullen. And what attraction did Grabben Gullen hold for me, you might ask...

Uncle John in his MG TD with Pauline.

CHAPTER NINE

Meeting Del

You might remember Kevin and Irene's wedding photo on the piano at Fern Hill, and how when I was thirteen I pointed out the flower girl, declaring my intention to marry her one day. Well, as crazy as it sounds, but that's actually what happened—and I have to thank Kevin and Irene for setting the wheels in motion.

Kevin & Irene's wedding photo.

I was seventeen at the time. Kevin and Irene were down from Wellington, just south of Dubbo, on holidays. They were going to a dance at Grabben Gullen, and asked me if I wanted to come. I said, 'Yes, I'd love to.' Kevin had a flash

Ford Fairlane ute, which suited me right down to the ground. There's nothing like arriving in style!

In the 1950's the main social activity in the country was the dances held most weekends. The local hall provided the venue—they were small halls and could hold about fifty people. There was usually a live pianist who played the piano to accompany the dances. The local country women served a delicious home-made supper usually consisting of sandwiches and cake, served with tea and coffee. The girls attending dressed beautifully in their dresses and we young men were all trussed up in suits, white shirts and shoes polished until you could see your face in them!

The custom was that the girls all sat inside the hall around the edges waiting to be asked to dance and all the men were over at the nearest hotel drinking beer until they had the courage to go inside and ask a girl to dance. The dances included waltzes, barn dances and various other old dances we all knew. Sometimes they included more modern dances like jitterbug and jive.

The pub at Grabben Gullen was only one hundred yards from the hall, and the barman didn't care who he served. So you'd have two or three beers to build up some courage, step outside to take a leak, then walk into the dance hall and set sail.

As soon as I walked in I noticed this fair girl with long wavy blonde hair sitting inside the hall. I could not believe how beautiful she looked. She knew who I was, because Kevin and Irene had visited her parents. I was the new boy, Kevin's nephew, even though I was only a few years younger than him. Let me tell you—the girls sussed you out as much as you sussed them out. They were whispering among themselves.

'Who's this young bloke?' 'I hear he's from Boorowa.' Anyway, I waltzed across the floor and asked her to dance.

To my surprise, she agreed.

I soon found out that her name was Del, and she was sixteen years old. She was wearing a rope skirt. Girls wore these skirts made of thin ropes sewed together, so when they swirled the skirt opened out, and you got a good look at their legs and bum. Del was a master of rock and roll, master of the jitterbug. Heel, toe, heel, toe, swirl. I was instantly smitten but thought I didn't have a hope in hell.

At those dances the girls usually had a chaperone with them to protect them from the less-than-wholesome intentions of the young men. Del's father always brought her to the dances and stayed outside the hall, keeping a close eye on her. If we went outside to the car, he quietly followed us, watching to ensure nothing inappropriate happened! Many of the other fathers drank while they waited, but Del's father never did.

I recall accompanying my own sisters to dances and acting in the same capacity to ensure their safety and decorum. As the men took more drink, fights sometimes broke out but always outside the hall.

In fact, I nearly got shot one night. I was there to look after my sister Pauline. There were some young men at the dance who were living at the racecourse. I had words with one of them, a real sleaze bag, about hanging around Pauline and after it got a bit heated we agreed to have a fight up at the racecourse. When I got up to the racecourse there was a group of them and one of them had a .22 rifle—I said to myself 'that's enough' and got out of there as quickly as possible! I was ready for a punch-up—not a shoot-up!

After the dance I walked Del over to her father's car. Because he was good friends with my uncle and aunt, he invited us back to his place for supper. Her mum made me a cup of tea and Sao biscuits topped with tomato. I was so nervous I squeezed the Sao too tight. It buckled in my hand and fell on the floor, right in the middle of my introduction to Del's family. So that's an evening I remember well!

When I got home Mum said, 'Did you meet anyone nice?'

I said I did, and told her about Del.

Mum asked me if her surname was Banfield. Then she told me that was the name of Kevin's flower girl.

Del and I met again at the next dance, where we danced together most of the night. We then just started going out together. Each fortnight I'd save up the money for petrol and booze. Del had to ask her father's permission. He was a hard taskmaster, always in the background. We'd go to the different dances around the district. I'd drive down to her farm and take her around. I've got photos of us at the Crookwell Show. We were smitten, for sure, from a very young age. The canoodling started pretty quick, I've got to admit. We have now been stepping out together for more than sixty years.

As you can imagine, I spent many hours on the road between Fern Hill and Grabben Gullen, visiting Del. It was a 45 mile drive between our two farms on a dusty road. Uncle John was kind enough to lend me his prized 1954 MG TD car on several occasions for the trip. Unfortunately, it had no petrol gauge and one cold night in the middle of nowhere it ran out of fuel. I could see a shearing shed in the distance and was able to suck the petrol of the engine there, siphon it into the car and got home safely. There was another night, also very cold, when a huge frost reminded me that I had no idea about how to put the hood on the car up. By the time I reached Fern Hill I was almost frozen.

When you're courting you want to look your best. I'd drive to within two miles of Del's house and pull up at the creek. I'd have a wash and make sure my hair was combed nicely. Looking back, I was a bit of a poof. I'd make sure my shoes were dust free and I'd arrive at Del's place looking all spic and span.

In the end, that fell in a heap. There was a family that live on a hill three-quarters of a mile away, and the two boys were a

Me at Fern Hill.

bit off, I must say. Their nicknames were Half and Quarter. I can't tell you why because it would be defamatory. They saw me at the creek making myself clean and tidy, and dobbed me in to Del's brother. I've always taken some pride in my appearance. I polished my shoes, my car, my motorbike. Everything shipshape and Bristol fashion. I'm still like that except I wear jeans all the time. They're comfortable and casual, but let's be honest—they're shearing trousers. Mum would say 'You're not going down the road in your shearing trousers, are you?'

She was prim and proper. She was still cleaning just before she died, in hospital. Del and I went to visit her and there she was, cleaning something at the edge of the bed. 'What are you doing Mum?' I said. There was nothing there.

'Unbelievable,' Del said. 'She's always cleaning.' Mind you,

Del at 17 years old & me at 19 and my way to Sydney to join the Police Force.

Del is always cleaning, too. She's even keener on cleaning than I am. So we fit together well in that regard.

It amazes me that I ever met Del. She lived in a different world to me. Her family was Methodist, while we were Catholic. Her parents were well-off, compared to mine. They lived forty miles away, which was a long distance in those days, along a dirt road filled with pothole and corrugations. Every time it rained the creeks would flood and cut them off. The road was so bad even cattle would object to walking down it.

Del and I were the same—we'd both left school early. Del left school earlier than she'd planned when her mother fell sick and had to go to Sydney for an operation. She became the shearer's cook on the family farm. Del was about fourteen years old at the time, in her second year of high school.

Later, Del worked on the telephone exchange at Crookwell. Every so often the police would come from Goulburn to raid the SP bookies in town. Someone would spot the coppers arriving, and ring the girls on the exchange, who'd immediately alert the bookies. The exchange was the lifeline of communication through the town, so the police never had a chance.

Me, I bloody detested school. Hated it. After I left school to go shearing I never went back. Del and I were both pleased to leave. They were great times, anything to get away from school.

However, I needed a job that would give me the freedom and money I needed to marry Del. So while we were courting, I moved to Sydney to begin training as a policeman.

CHAPTER TEN

The Police Force

I started thinking of joining the police force when I was around seventeen, but at that age I would have had to go in as a cadet. Time rolled on and I was able to join without a cadetship when I was nineteen so I joined up in 1954. My main inspiration was Jack Sparkes, the copper back home. He was a decent bloke, and I thought if I could be like him, I'd do all right. Mind you, I was worried that my lack of education might be a problem. I also didn't know if there was any record of me pinching the cake!

I went along to the recruitment office, completed the required exercises which included a maths test involving a long division calculation of pounds shillings and pence, a written exercise and my height and weight were measured. To my surprise, I got through the English test, but failed the long division. Long division is a bloody mongrel of a thing to work out. Then you add pounds, shillings and pence just to make it more difficult.

I had a piece of foolscap paper to work on, and by the time I was down to ha'pennies and farthings I'd reached the bottom of the page. Having left school early to go rabbiting, mining and shearing meant my mathematical knowledge deserted me. I failed dismally. My brain wouldn't click at all.

Because I had passed the rest, they said I could come back the next morning to have another crack at the long division.

They also suggested that I find someone who could help me learn.

I went home that night and asked my Great Auntie Em to help me. She was Ralph's wife. She said 'I'll help you, I'm not that good at it myself, but I'll show you.' She was some sort of artist, probably a bullshit artist, but she was an arty sort of person. She set to and as soon as she started to show me it all came back. I was good at maths, no doubt in the world, because it all came back to me. All you needed to do was work through the right sequence and you'd have so many shillings left over and so on.

So I came back the next day, sat in the room by myself, and passed with flying colours.

I also needed to make weight, because I was six feet tall and needed to be twelve stone. So I ate a bunch of bananas over the preceding days to make the minimum weight, and was accepted. I now believe that nobody is responsible at that age. In my year as a police officer, I never booked anyone—I felt too much of a hypocrite and it was a relief when I left.

We undertook three months of training at Bourke Street in Sydney, learning about the law, powers of arrest and going to watch proceedings in the local courts. After our initial training, we had to return to college one night each week for a while. Seeing the court process really made me nervous, the thought of appearing in court terrified me and I have never enjoyed speaking in public. It became clear to me fairly early in my service that the Police force was not for me, but I was proud that I completed my training, I thought that was a good result for a country lad with little formal education.

When we graduated we had no idea about where we might be posted—I thought I would be posted to the motor bike squad. We were measured up and a month later were fitted out in our made-to-measure uniforms. The uniform included starched detachable collars, which I hated wearing with a passion because the starched collars rubbed my short neck raw. As my uniform included jodhpurs and leggings, my conviction that I was heading towards the bike squad grew—but I was delighted when I was appointed to the horse squad.

One of the awkward moments I remember from my training was sitting in court observing and recognising a woman charged with prostitution offences—she had been known to me as the cook at the Frogmore mining camp! I sank down in my seat as low as possible in the hope she would not recognise me. If she did see me, there was no flicker of recognition. That could have taken some explaining.

We received a lot of training with firearms and we carried guns, semiautomatics. The guns we used were Luger, I think, and were very hard to cock and then once cocked were automatic which makes one nervous. We also had to learn unarmed combat which I thought was a bit of light relief—I knew from my earlier boxing training that the techniques we were taught were ineffectual. We also carried fixed solid batons and handcuffs.

As I have said, I never arrested anyone—it seemed wrong given some of my youthful escapades. I certainly did not want to go to court to give evidence. I also remember a neighbour from Boorowa brazenly asking me 'to get him a good watch' when I arrested someone and he was quite serious. I was shocked and enraged by his request but it also confused me—I was still trying to fathom out the ways of the world at that age.

As a policeman, my day started with horse work in Centennial Park with the horse squad at 7.00 AM. Strange

Me in Police uniform. Sworn in on May 10th, 1955.

as it may sound, given my background, I didn't enjoy the working with horses. It was totally different to what I expected. I was nineteen years old and I'd had my fill of horses. I'd been riding them since I was four or five. The way they treated the horses was ridiculous. They used to polish their feet, lift their tail and wipe their arse out with a wet bag, and wipe their nostrils. If they had too much green on their teeth you had to get that off if you could. You have got to be kidding—this wasn't how I was brought up with horses.

I went from being a bush boy on a bush horse to being a city boy on a highly groomed horse. They groomed them like thoroughbreds. In fact, a lot of them were ex-racehorses. Not 100%, but probably 90%. They would feed them less oats, because oats make them prickly. They'd bring them down to a quieter horse. They had to be quiet otherwise they'd be kicking the shit out of people when the coppers were directing traffic on pedestrian crossings.

The copper in charge of the mounted police, Sergeant Livermore, was a real old dick. A real shocker. He seemed to pick on me because I could ride a horse. He had a bunch of city kids there who couldn't ride, and of course I jumped straight on the horse. You'd think he might have some respect for you if you could ride, but he didn't. Trouble is, I didn't ride like a little ponce. I learned to ride a horse to do bush work, and to ride all day. Number one is to stay in the saddle. Sergeant Livermore wanted his boys to sit straight and tall, so they ended up looking like Little Lord Fauntleroys, the lot of them. If their horse shied they'd be gone. They wouldn't be able to recover.

So each time I rode the horse I'd have this old sergeant growling at me. 'Dromgold. Your mother will know you when we go on parade because you're the only bloke who's sitting up there like that!' So I didn't like him and he didn't like me, which is fair enough.

After the horse work I'd go back to the barracks and do some pistol shooting. I found cocking those old Ruger pistols was hard. They were semi-automatic so once you'd cocked it you were away. They'd make you balance a sixpence on the barrel and shoot at a target. You were supposed to keep the sixpence from falling off. It wasn't easy. But I felt good doing it. I loved shooting, but I'd rather be shooting at live targets. We always had guns on the farm.

After that I'd do my beat. I started out at the old Darlinghurst Police Station just off the top of Oxford Street, in Taylor Square. So I'd walk down Oxford Street and turn right into College, then along to the Australian Museum on the corner of William Street. By the time I got to the museum I was almost halfway through my beat, so I'd go around the back where the curators were working. They were decent blokes, and they'd be hard at work preparing their displays. I got to know them a little, and they didn't seem to mind having a yarn with a copper.

I remember watching them stuff a kookaburra once. They made it look so lifelike. Taxidermy is a really specialised art.

They were qualified people. When I was watching I'd realised I'd rather be stuffing kookaburras than being a policeman.

I also saw them preparing a crocodile skin. They dried it out and treated it with formaldehyde. I'd spend maybe twenty to thirty minutes there. I went in there to get out of the road. Hiding away. You never knew who was watching you on the street. A sergeant or someone might come around in plain clothes. In those days if you met a higher rank—and they were all higher than me—you had to salute them. I wasn't up for that. I never really got the gist of all that saluting.

So then I'd head up to the five-ways at the Cross, which has since been changed to four-ways. One day I was directing traffic there. A nineteen year old country boy—I was completely overwhelmed with the cars coming at me from all those different directions. My responsibility for smooth traffic flow and ensuring everyone had their opportunity to get through the intersection overwhelmed me. I panicked and walked off the street, leaving them to work it out for themselves! There were no ramifications.

I also recall directing traffic in Oxford Street in Sydney at a busy major intersection and feeling a light touch on my palm. Reflexively, I closed my fingers and continued directing traffic only to discover that some larrikin had shoved a newspaper into my hand and then disappeared, leaving me directing traffic and waving a newspaper around. Believe me, I felt pretty stupid.

So after doing such a sterling job of managing Sydney's traffic, I'd cut back across to the top of Oxford Street to the police station. The sergeant might tell me to fingerprint someone, or just undertake general duties. For all my dreams about becoming a policeman, it just wasn't me. I didn't take to it at all.

At the time I was sharing accommodation in Newtown with another officer, Brian, the two Brians. He was a funny bugger. A good soccer player, physically fit, with a nice family that lived down at Coledale, a bit north of Wollongong. He and I had travelled down by train to visit them on a couple of weekends. His old man was a coal miner. Our flat had a fireplace and one night he went out after complaining about how cold the flat was. Shortly afterwards, he returned with a number of old and rotten fence palings under his arm! We were then able to warm ourselves over the fire. Brian seemed like a nice guy but that wasn't how he turned out.

Actually, at that time I was trying to court Del and needed to have two consecutive days off to get to Crookwell and back by public transport. My sergeant in charge always refused to allow leave for consecutive days unless you had a medical certificate.

In this case, Del was sick. She had her appendix out, so I hopped on the train and went to Crookwell. While I was absent without leave, Brian decided to impersonate me. He got dressed up in my leggings and jodhpurs, went across to the Watson Bay Hotel, and got into a fight. The shit hit the fan and they traced the gear he was wearing. He wasn't supposed to be wearing those trousers because he wasn't in the Horse Squad. At first they thought I'd sanctioned him to wear them, but I hadn't.

So when I returned I was called in by my superiors, including my inspector, to be questioned about an 'incident' in which I had been allegedly involved. At first, they didn't tell me what Brian had done. This was the catalyst for my resignation. I was so pissed off with Brian that I never saw him again. I resigned, leaving with an unblemished record.

Brian Dromgold

Brian later had his employment as a police officer terminated. Thus ended my career as a police officer.

CHAPTER ELEVEN

James R. Conduit Pty. Ltd.

Soon after leaving the police, I obtained employment at 56 York Street, Sydney, with a company called James R. Conduit Pty. Ltd. I applied for work not really knowing what the job entailed but assuming my previous experience working with electrical conduits in the mines would be relevant. Imagine my amazement when my interviewer, Mr. Crow, explained their business was manufacturing straw hats for women and I was to be responsible for the packing and dispatch of all of the finished hats! My first thought was that this was not for me and I said as much, but agreed to give it a try. I stayed there for approximately three years.

It was a busy place. Again, I worked a double shift—daytime hours at the factory arranging dispatch to the major department stores of the day like Myer Emporium, David Jones and Foy's and then taking the hats home at night, by the carload, hats that needed wire put into them and finishing them. Del and I worked together on this. She'd feed the wire through, I'd bend it and cut it off. As a result we made some additional income working at piece rates.

There were 76 women working for James R. Conduit, and only a handful of men. There was the owner, who had his own office. You didn't see much of him. He shared the ownership with a woman who ran a good portion of the business. There was a bloke named Crowe, I can't recall his first name, who attended to guests. He had a little lounge where clients could look at a range of sample hats.

Then there was Norm, who always dressed immaculately in a bow tie. He'd visit the department stores in Sydney, Melbourne and even Brisbane, and take orders for thousands of hats. He'd take his samples around and come back with orders for two dozen of this and eighteen of that. He'd give the orders to the woman in charge first, then pass them on to me to fulfil.

As well as packing the hats in tissue paper and managing the dispatch of orders, I also prepared invoices, and kept track of the different hats as they made their way through the production line. Pieces of felt or straw would come into the factory, be steamed and shaped on hat-blocks, and transformed into something women could wear to the races.

James R. Conduit had two different divisions: ready to wear, and models. The ready to wears were cheap little things that women would use every day when they went out. The models were more expensive, more lavish. They were cut from sisal, steam and shaped, then decorated with ribbons and other frills. There were also odd hats made from felt. The seniors were responsible for all the decoration.

One thing I will say about working in a roomful of women was that it was very nice! They knew that I was engaged to Del and they all chipped in to give us a wedding present. In those days everyone would put in two bob and buy you an iron or a toaster. However, some of them did come on to me—there were a couple of girls who liked to flirt and tease—but I held them off. I resisted. I only had eyes for Del.

One morning when I came into work I must have looked a little downcast, because Crowe asked me what the trouble was. I said, 'I've got a bloody boil on my dick.' Unbeknownst to me he went and whispered to the woman who I mentioned before, the part owner. She said 'I'll take him home. We'll soon fix that up!'

I realised women can be wild and crude. After that I never told them anything.

Not all the women were easy to work with. There was one old dragon on the staff who worked on the switchboard. She listened in to all my calls with Del. Every time we spoke I knew she was on the line. She was an absolute shocker. Back then, you'd have called her vinegar tits. Of course, you wouldn't say that these days, because we're all grown up, but back then we weren't so fussy.

The dragon also checked my invoices before we sent them out. Because I came from the bush and had a very poor education, I had a battle to sort things out. Invoicing didn't come easy to me. I had to make sure the amounts were right. Tally it all up in pounds, shillings and pence. So you might have ten hats at seventeen pounds twenty-four pence two shillings and a threepence halfpenny. I struggled with that but I never got bawled out over any mistakes, so I can't have been too bad. Myers and the other stores would check the invoice at their end and adjust it anyway. So everything was double-checked.

I was a little bit of a suave character when I was working there. I'd go to work in a suit, sometimes a bow tie, and a little hat. Very dapper. However, that image didn't suit me. It was just what the company expected. Not that my looks were anything to rave about.

One time when Norm Biddulph was sick they sent me on his sales round. I met the main buyers in David Jones, Myers, Mark Foy's, and McDowell's up in Oxford Street. I was definitely being groomed for a sales position. If I had stayed, that's where I would have ended up. But a few years later, people stopped wearing hats, and the whole business closed down. So if I stayed, I'd have been left high and dry.

As it was, I gave a good three years of my life to the hat industry. I enjoyed it. For the first time, I felt as though I was making a contribution to Sydney. During that time, I also had a 'milk run'. This was my joking reference to my lunch time deliveries, for my sister Pauline, of milk she had expressed for her premature baby, Debbie, at Camperdown hospital. I brought the expressed milk to work, stored it in the refrigerator then in my lunch hour delivered the milk to the hospital.

A cousin of mine talked me into joining the Fire Brigade. At first, I wasn't sure, but my cousin's girlfriend's father was a fire chief in Castlereagh Street. I went and had a yarn to him. He said put in an application. He gave me the forms, I filled them in, lodged them, and to my surprise they accepted me, I got in and away I went.

However, it was while I was working in the hat trade that Del and I tied the knot. So let's travel back to Crookwell to celebrate the happy event.

CHAPTER TWELVE

Our Wedding

I was surprised when Del accepted my proposal for marriage, because I wasn't sure she was going to accept. She was her own person and a flipping Methodist. I came from the wrong side of the tracks, from a wild Catholic family. While Del agreed, our parents didn't. My father was a bigot as a Catholic and Del's father was a bigot as a Protestant!

My Uncle John took me to the back of the woolshed and asked me, 'What do you want to bloody go and marry a Methodist for?' I replied 'Uncle John, I've only got to look around and see all the Catholics, they go to the pub, they get drunk, they're all bloody hopeless—including Dad'. I told him that when I went down to Del's place there was no alcohol in the house. Now that was a bit of a lie. Del's father kept a sneaky bottle of whiskey in the cupboard for the winter lambing. July and August get bitterly cold in Crookwell so a man has to do whatever he can to stay warm.

After I explained myself, Uncle John said, 'Fair enough.' At the time, I said that to him to appease him and because his approval was important to me. I was a bit hypocritical saying that as I also resorted to the amber fluid from time to time before marrying Del. The truth is that there were elements of the Catholics who drank too much, including Dad, but there were also many men who took a drink occasionally and were unaffected by it.

Boorowa had a well-deserved reputation as being a wild lawless town, renowned for its fighting and drinking. There were a lot of Irish Catholics and there was a real divide between the Catholics and Protestants—even the cemetery had a fence between the two religions!

While Uncle John accepted my decision, Dad bucked and screamed and went on and bloody on about it. My grandmother—Dad's mother—was none too happy either. These religious differences can twist a family about. Because I was just under the legal marrying age, I needed parental permission. Initially, Dad tried to withhold his consent and we had a confrontation. He said he wouldn't go to the wedding and I told him if he didn't sign the papers I'd wait an extra month until I was twenty-one and get married then. I was calling his bluff. Del wanted to get married on Easter Saturday so I really didn't want to postpone the wedding. Anyway, Dad agreed to it in the finish. While he relented, but his mother and his side of the family refused to attend. Dad attended reluctantly, but my mother's side and their families all came. We had a fine wedding regardless of the religious tensions.

Mind you, Dad could still be stubborn when he chose. We held Diane's christening in the Methodist church at Crookwell—went back especially for it—but Dad refused to come. He was a bloody hypocrite because he never went to church. He'd drive us seventeen miles to go to mass at Boorowa and he'd head off to the pub instead. He was an alcoholic, so he thought about the booze more than anything else.

Del had the same problem as me. Her father didn't really want her to marry me. He was further up the social scale than us. When Del was little they had a maid when her mother fell sick. A maid—that was unheard of at our place. There were some very well-to-do graziers in the Crookwell district—the

Kensits and the Kellys—and Del's father hoped she would marry one of their sons. But she never showed any interest in them. Instead, she chose me, which was good!

Del and I got engaged when we went to Goulburn, 28 miles from her farm, and bought the ring. We went back to the farm as happy as Larry. Dels' father wasn't so happy when we made our announcement. He took the ring off her, announced that we were disengaged, and handed the ring back to me. As far as he was concerned, I was a bit of a lair, taking his daughter off to Goulburn and squiring around in a sports jacket.

Despite what her father said, Del and I still considered ourselves engaged. I put the ring in a box and put the box in the pocket of my sports jacket. The weather in Sydney was too hot for the jacket, so I put it in at the dry cleaners. I was devastated when realised what I'd done. I was in the police force at that stage, renting a place in Newtown. We didn't have any money to speak of, and I'd spent most of what I had on that ring. Lucky for me the dry cleaners were honest. They rang the police station in Bourke Street to let me know they'd found the ring. Of course, being a copper might have helped. Del still wears that ring today. She's had it remodelled to fit with her other rings.

While we were courting, Del and I talked about our different religious upbringings. After she agreed to marry me, I asked to hold the ceremony in the Catholic church. Again, she agreed. I was unimpressed with the power religion held over people at the time, so then I said I'd marry her in the Methodist church. I wasn't serious about my religion. From the age of twelve I couldn't give two hoots about it. So when I asked Del to marry me in the Catholic church I was being a little nasty. Trying it on, you know?

Jack was the best man at my wedding. I didn't see Del for three or four days before the wedding, maybe a week. I was at Boorowa, while she was at Grabben Gullen. We talked on the phone. I was nervous, wondering if she was going to turn up! Of course I knew she was going to, but there's always nerves before you get married, aren't there?

The night before the wedding Jack and a few of us had a buck's party. There were four pubs and two clubs in Boorowa back then, and we hit them all. There were maybe six or seven of us. We ended up heading out of town a mile where the council workers had pitched their tent. They stayed in the tent overnight while they were working on the road. We snuck up and let the ropes down on their tent while they were sleeping. We just bolted. They probably knew who it was. Boorowa was an Irish town. They'd just think we were stupid bastards.

Then we went around to Leo Polodis's café and banged on the door. He yelled out for us to go away, he was closed. Eventually he opened up and cooked us all a steak. We'd been going there for years, so he was OK with us in the end.

After our late supper we went back to our hotel and crashed. The next morning I felt pretty shady, let me tell you. I couldn't even put my tie on. I had to get jack to help. I'd had a few drinks but that wasn't the problem. I was just so nervous.

It was Easter Saturday on 31 March, 1956. We headed off to the Methodist church in Crookwell for the wedding at five o'clock that evening. It was a perfect day, with the sun just setting.

Up the front of the church I was too nervous to move. Jack was calm. He had no nerves at all. He could make a speech about anyone or anything at any time. He's just babble on like a country boy. I could never do that. You need the gift of the gab speak that way.

Dad came to our wedding. I wanted him there and I also didn't want him there. One sip of beer and he'd be away. So I was hoping he wouldn't get drunk and spoil things for us.

Uncle John was a red-hot Catholic, so it was good of him to come to a Methodist church for my wedding. I expected him to be there because he was such an important part of our family. When Del walked in the door I saw her, and I saw Uncle John with his white hair standing up all over the place. I couldn't help it. I wept. Del wept. We were both so happy.

Our wedding on March 31st, 1956. Jack Elkins, my sister Pauline, Maree Banfield (Del's cousin), me, Del & Les Banfield (Del's Dad).

Del copped some flak from one of her aunties for betraying her faith. Aunt Selma—she was one of the hard hitters—said our marriage wouldn't last. Forty-five years later we were at Del's Uncle Col's funeral. Del siddled up to Selma. Selma said, 'I've got to admit I was wrong.' Selma and Col owned

Me & Del at a colleague's 21st party not long after our wedding.

the house at Elanora. He became a ranger, so they didn't need the house. We rented it at first and then we bought it off them.

After the wedding, Del's father leant us his brand new Holden, so we could drive from Crookwell up to Goulburn. There, we caught a train to Katoomba, for our honeymoon.

Honeymoon in Katoomba

I always said when I got married I felt like I'd gone heaven. After the wedding we travelled by train to Katoomba for our honeymoon. I felt so proud of my beautiful bride as we walked from Katoomba Station down to The Cecil in Lurline Street. Del was wearing her going away dress made from steel-grey fabric, with her matching hat, gloves and handbag. I struggled along behind her, carrying two suitcases, a hat box and a beauty case. The Cecil was an old place, so I don't remember much about the décor. It was an old romantic building like you'd see in England, except it was made out of weatherboards. Anyway, I didn't travel to Katoomba to look at the architecture. Del had my full attention.

The next morning at about eight o'clock I woke up, pulled back the curtains, and saw the fog drifting across the mountains and valleys. 'I didn't dream it,' I told myself, 'I really am in heaven.' This mist would stay in the bottom of the valley all day, but it cleared at the top.

Katoomba is a spectacular location. The Three Sisters at Echo Point are the town's most famous attraction. They jut out into Jamison Valley, and it's a drop of one thousand feet from the lookout down to the valley floor. The whole romance of our honeymoon added fuel to the fire, but Katoomba was incredibly beautiful. Just like Del, in fact!

We had an interesting coincidence when we went down to the dining room for diner. Ruth, a girl I had worked with in the Conduit Hat Company was holidaying in Katoomba with her husband. It was lovely to have them as company, rather than a bunch of strangers. We went to the Jenolan Caves, which required a bus ride over some shocking roads. Steep descents, with the road base washed away and the dirt crumbling. An old bus with no seat belts, the driver double declutching as he went down through the gears. Being born and bred in the bush I'm used to some terrible roads, but this was as hairy as anything.

They also had busses that ran around the top of Katoomba, taking you to all the different lookouts. There was a scenic railway as they called it that goes down almost vertically, from the top of the cliff down to the bottom of the valley. It runs on rails but it's pulled up and down by cables. You're dropping down over one thousand feet at an angle of 52 degrees. And when you get to the bottom you've got to strap in again to get back to the top! That frightened the crap out of me.

We had good fun together on that honeymoon. We did a lot of walking. As a tennis and hockey player, Del was really fit, which was just as well with all those hills. We wore out our sandshoes with all the walking. We didn't talk much about the future. We didn't worry where we were going to live. Del had provided most of the money for the honeymoon. She was a good saver. I'd spend my money of flowers and gifts for her. We were just so deeply in love we couldn't worry about the future. We knew something would crop up.

Even though we never had any money, things weren't as tough in those days. We thought we'd rent a place when we got back to Sydney. Del's parents were worried, so they rang some people they knew who had holiday apartments in Manly, at 24 East Esplanade. They booked a room for us so we'd have somewhere to live after the honeymoon. I guess I was pretty slack not to have lined up somewhere to live.

One thing we talked about was babies. Del wanted to have kids but we didn't want them straight away. We agreed we needed somewhere to live first!

After we returned to Manly we moved into that room at East Esplanade. The shower was downstairs, and we had to put two shilling coins into the meter to operate the hot water system. When the money ran out, so did the hot water!

Del loved Manly. When she was younger her family would holiday at Manly each year. When Uncle John and I came down to Sydney for the Easter Show, we'd always catch the ferry out to Manly. We'd have fish and chips and a look around. You'd walk along the Corso with the harbour at one end and the surf at the other. Back then, Manly was very laid back. It was just a seaside village, nothing over two stories high. Remember the old saying? *Seven miles from Sydney and a thousand miles from care.*

It was very convenient. You could catch the ferry in to Circular Quay, and then you had trains that ran everywhere—Sydney Town Hall, Wynyard, you name it. I was working in 56 York Street at the time and I always enjoyed the ferry ride back at the end of the day.

There was one ferry trip I'll always remember, when my sister was staying with us at Elanora Heights. I was taking her back to Central Station, to put her on the train to Boorowa. The winds came up and the harbour was so choppy that her suitcase got away from me and I couldn't catch it. It kept sliding up and down. The ferry would poke its nose right up in the air, and then all of a sudden there'd be nothing supporting it, and BANG, she'd smash down and the water would flood over the bow. Nasty! That was the last ferry to or from Manly that day—they cancelled the service until the weather settled. I had to catch a bus all the way back around to Manly to pick up my car.

Del and I only stayed briefly at East Esplanade. We then rented a house on the peak at Collaroy, overlooking Long Reef golf course. On one side of the road there's the golf course and the ocean; on the other side there's all these flash houses. We rented the underneath of one of those houses. It had a beautiful view of the fairways and the surf. We did stupid things. Just for the hell of it, we bought a box of chocolates, ate them all, and threw the wrappers around the room. That wasn't in either of our natures. But we were free, and enjoying that freedom for the first time in our lives. We were saying, 'We can do this if I want to. There's no one to tell us off. We're our own boss!'

Long Reef was a renowned rock-fishing spot. I had a close call fishing off those rocks one day with a mate. We had set up all our fishing gear on the rocks noting that the waves were breaking at least four feet below us—we had our cigarettes with our gear and suddenly without warning a huge wave broke right over the top of the rock, and we were in waist deep water being swept out to sea as the waves surged around us. Fortunately, we were strong enough swimmers to swim through the swell and make it back to the rocks safely but of course we had lost all our gear and tobacco to the ocean. I relive that experience every time I hear media stories about people being washed off rocks—we were just lucky.

Our next home was to be at Elanora Heights, the house we bought from Selma and Col. But before I move on to our life at Elanora Heights, and my career with the Fire Brigade, Del would like a few words:

> *I was blessed with wonderful parents. I lived with them in Grabben Gullen until Brian and I married. Dad had a farm at Dalton, about twenty-eight kilometres from where we lived. I grew up with my sister Dawn and my two brothers. Dawn passed away after a lifetime of suffering from severe epilepsy. Brian and I looked after Dawn, visited her and set her up in a unit where she could live independently.*
>
> *One of the common childhood experiences I share with Brian is that, as a child, I also rabbited, with my brother Barry. There was a rabbit plague on at that time and so we blocked a hole in the fence they climbed through and we would just kill them with a stick as they tried to get through the fence. We threaded their legs together and brought them home to Dad to skin and peg them. The skin man paid for them and it was a good income for us. We were lucky that Dad let us keep the money.*
>
> *Barry passed away last year quite suddenly when I was in hospital and I missed the chance to say my farewells to him—I miss him greatly.*

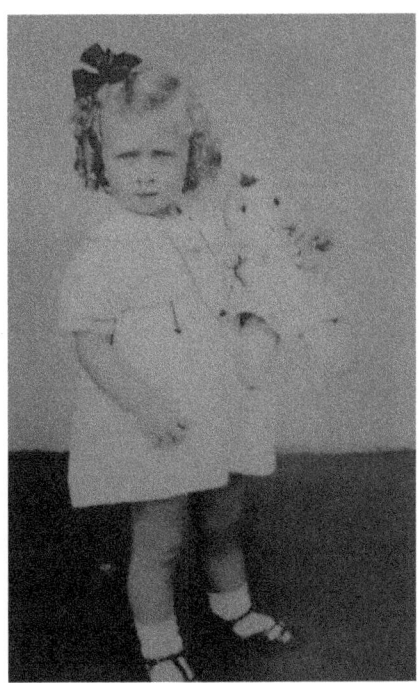

Del at 10 months & Del's mother.   Del at 3 years old.

Barry & Ross – Del's brothers.

Del at 6 years old   Del at 8 years old & Barry at 6.

It is hard for people today to understand what a rabbit plague was like. At night with a light you could see a whole paddock moving and writhing and it was wall to wall rabbits. They were so destructive, not only did they eat the crops but all their burrowing undermined paddocks and it was very costly for farmers to undo the damage they caused. There were farmers who tried to fill the burrows in so the rabbits died in them.

From when I turned sixteen, I went to the local dances, which were held most weekends, once each month. My mother made me a new dress for every dance and helped me look my best, which were very important social events in our calendar. They provided an opportunity for us to enjoy dancing, a chance for the local country women to prepare and provide a supper of lovely cakes and sandwiches with tea and coffee and the lady who played the piano played beautifully. It saddens me to think that the dances no longer exist.

My father took me to the dances and sat outside until the dance finished, when he walked me back to his car. He was very protective of me. A number of the fathers were present and filled the time drinking—my father did not take a drink as his focus was to ensure my safety.

Sometimes fights broke out among the men waiting outside— but never in the hall. I always felt safe with Dad there, watching over me, even when scuffles broke out.

I loved the dancing. One night I noticed a handsome, smartly dressed man come into the hall. My first thought was that I had never seen him before and how good looking he was. Then the music began, he came over and asked me to dance and now Brian and I have been dancing together for more than sixty years. At the end of the night he escorted me back to

Del on Stumpy – check the stirrups!

Del at 16 years old as we headed off to the Crookwell show.

Dad's car. As Dad was friendly with Brian's aunt and uncle, they came back to our home, with Brian, for a cup of tea and that was the beginning.

I am still friends with a girl who started school with me aged five and who was at that dance. She still laughs as she describes watching Brian come into the hall that night, see me as the music began and head straight towards me to ask me to dance without a sidelong glance at any other girl in the hall! I later heard from his family the story about

Del's family at Crookwell.

his declaration that he would marry 'the girl in the photo' which stood on his mother's piano.

Several years before Brian and I met I had been a flower girl when Brian's Uncle had married and I was the mysterious 'girl in the photo'. I think it is like a lovely magic tale. I do believe that when things are meant to be they will prevail. Brian and I chuckle about that still—he recently gently chided an aunt of mine, reminding her that she prophesied that our marriage would never last and here we were in our sixtieth year of marriage.

I was eighteen when Brian proposed to me, but my parents would not allow it. However, Dad could see Brian was a good man and permitted us to marry. Ever since the day of our wedding, we have never had a fight or cross words. Brian has always been a kind man and a very good worker. He has been a good provider and helped me in every possible way when we had three small children—I believe that we were just destined to be together.

Del's parents – Ena & Les Banfield

Our different religions caused some tension, especially with Brian's father. He threatened to boycott our wedding and later refused to attend Diane's christening when we took her back to the church in Crookwell for it.

The best decision we made after our marriage was to move to Sydney—away from our families so that we could forge our own way. Many of our relatives predicted our marriage would not last. After we left Manly and moved to Elanora Heights, I started work and we waited three years before having children.

After Brian and I married, Mum and Dad visited us quite often. Although I missed them, I always knew we had made the best decision in choosing to make our own way.

My first job was on an assembly line for an electrical company making household fittings—it was terribly monotonous. My next work was as a telephonist for the Melbourne Steamship

Del on Bondi Beach.   Me on Bondi Beach.

Company—work I loved. I had been a telephonist in Crookwell and enjoyed talking to people and had no difficulty juggling the lines on the switchboard—up to six at one time.

I recall that, when I was interviewed, I was asked my religion. When I replied 'Methodist', I was immediately appointed. At that time, everyone employed there was Methodist which created a sense of community. They never found out that Brian was Catholic!

I worked at the Steamship Company for three years before becoming pregnant. So Brian worked two jobs for the next twelve years to support the family while I looked after the babies. They were beautiful babies, although one of them kept us on our toes.

Diane was an easy baby and child and a conscientious worker and student. She started paid work as soon as she could and she gave us no trouble. She liked books, was an indoors girl and was a bit of a shadow of mine around the house, when she was small.

She married very young and it was a great sadness for her and us when her husband's behaviour changed and he began hurting her to the point where she called on us to help her to move out, which we willingly did. We were very clear that she could not return to his abuse. She stayed with us until she got back on her feet but it was a great shock for her—he seemed to change his nature completely and became a horrible beast. Happily, she came through that time and now lives in Sydney with her lovely partner. Her great passion in life is her career and Brian and I supported that and are extremely proud of her achievements. She had a lot of friends and they had similar interests to her—they wanted to go to university too and they have all succeeded in their chosen fields.

Christine was a baby who did not sleep well, she cried and screamed quite a bit. I can remember Brian helping me with Christine, pushing her stroller with his foot while we tried to sleep and she would scream each time he stopped. Once my father came down from the country and said 'give her to me—I'll look after her'– but after half an hour he brought her back to me and handed her back saying 'you'll have to have her back—I can't do anything with her!'

As she grew up, she was mischievous, and was very spirited. Brian's father always called her the wild one. Christine was a great athlete and represented the ACT in several sports. I think sport helped her to channel her energy. Christine has three children we love to bits. They often visit us and come and go in our home as though it's their own. Christine is very strong, very capable and has done a wonderful job of raising her children. In recent years Christine has been the one we call when we need help.

Sometimes in the middle of the night, she is always the one who comes running. We are very grateful for her support and her sense of humour—which is really good, she can keep us all laughing for hours.

Richard came along with a quiet gentle nature, and is still the same. Brian was happy to have a son and ecstatic when Richard had four boys, so the name will be carried on. I spent a lot of time looking after Richard's boys when their mother was ill. The boys were close in age and they were busy times for me. I love those beautiful boys and I like to think they love me too.

Brian was happy for me to attend the religious upbringing of our children as I was a devout Methodist and he was working so hard. When I was in my paid work in telephony, I started to work with computers and new technology but then found I was tired and started to question whether I really needed to keep working. I wanted to be able to help Christine and Richard (who both lived in Canberra) with their children, particularly when they were sick and needed to be cared for while parents had to work. With looking after grandchildren, our home and Brian, I felt I could stop working.

I finished work in 1995 as the technology was changing everything. Now we simply call on a grandchild when we need technological assistance!

We were very fortunate in our marriage as we were each able to do the things we liked best—I prefer the 'inside' work and Brian likes the 'outside' work so we worked well together. In any relationship I feel it is important to be tolerant and understanding, to be kind to each other, not to dwell on things—sometimes it is necessary to look the other way. Brian and I have not had a fight in our sixty years of marriage. Brian is a dream to live with and is very easy to look after—in fact in recent times he has been looking after me with my health challenges, including recuperating from hip replacement surgery.

Brian back again. Isn't my wife the loveliest person? I think so. Now, let me tell you about my years with the Fire Brigade, in Sydney's northern beaches.

CHAPTER THIRTEEN

The Fire Brigade

I'll always remember my first call-out as a fire officer.

It was at Dee Why on Sydney's northern beaches—between Manly and Palm Beach. I could feel my heart racing as I scrambled to board the fire engine. There is always an adrenaline hit when you head out to a fire—bells ring in the station and everyone moves quickly and then the sirens blare out. As you approach the fire, you never know what you're going to find.

In this case, the house—little more than a shanty, in fact—was burnt-out by the time we arrived. The building had fallen in, and I could tell at a glance it had been poorly built. A real fire trap. Fires have different smells—bush, rubber, grass, house fittings. These smells had me and my mate working our way around the property, raking at debris with our fireman's axes. The axe had a blade for cutting and a point for lifting debris. We were surrounded by smoke and the stench of burned materials grabbed us by the throat and refused to let go. Had the house been occupied? We had no idea.

Methodically, we moved through the ruins. I punched my axe into a sheet of iron and ripped it upwards. Human intestines spilled out—I had stumbled upon the remains of one of the residents who had died in the fire. I started vomiting at that moment and rushed out to the edge of the property. I bent over, put my hands on my knees, and spewed my heart out until I couldn't spew any more. Then I went back in. It's not like I had any choice.

After all, I was twenty-three years old. I wasn't going to let anyone see me snivelling in the corner over something as insignificant as a charred corpse. We were all like that, me and my mates. We toughed it out. We never thought how these emotional calluses might affect us later on in life.

Not that I went near the body. That became a matter for the police. Once they started their examination they took it out of your hands. Mind you, they couldn't enter the site until we'd given them the all-clear. You wouldn't want some copper wandering through the wreckage and having a smouldering beam knock him on the head. Then you'd have another corpse to be worrying about.

So here's the thing I learned on my first call-out: that burnt human flesh smells like roast pork. That memory baked into my nose and into my soul, if you believe in such things. I vomited constantly for the next two weeks. It was like the morning after a heavy night on the tiles, but the hangover lingered for a fortnight.

Even once I'd done with the throwing up, I couldn't stand the smell of pork cooking on the stove. It took me right back to that moment at Dee Why. Years would pass before I could cope with the smell of seared pork. I couldn't eat the stuff. Even though I knew it was a piece of pork on the plate and not a human body, a sympathetic nerve took over. I just couldn't eat it.

I didn't discuss this with anyone. The fire brigade didn't have people you could lean on, cry on their shoulders or anything like that. You just wore it. Everyone expected you to be the big brave fireman. You didn't talk about it with your mates at the station, either. You were expected to do your job and that was it.

How did we cope? Some blokes hit the grog. But I never drank to any extent. Sure, I'd had a few grogs before I got married. But once I was married I couldn't afford it. Until we moved to Canberra in 1969, I hardly drank any grog at all. It may sound strange now, but back then there weren't many grog outlets in Sydney. In Canberra you could buy grog at the post office! We went back to Manly for a holiday a few years after we moved to Canberra. I had to walk three-quarters of a mile to the nearest pub to buy two stubbies. I couldn't believe it. I'd forgotten how hard it was to buy alcohol in Sydney in the 1960s.

I always had my father's example in the back of my mind. He'd get so loaded he couldn't scratch himself. Although I didn't know then that alcoholism was a disease, I never wanted to be in that position. Even though I never had an addictive nature, I did get addicted to cough medicine as a fourteen-year-old.

I was working out in the paddock and if I had a bit of a tickle in my throat I'd take a sip of Bonnington's Irish Moss. Made me feel pretty good. Then I realised I was still sipping the stuff even though the cold had cleared up. That made me stop right away.

In the back of my mind I've never wanted to lose control of my faculties. I've been on jobs where there's always been some idiot who picks on the weakest in the group. If I'm sober I know I can talk my way out of trouble, or punch my way if it comes to that.

Anyway, back to the fire brigade. I had my way of dealing with the stress. If it got too bad I went fishing. The station was just a stone's throw from the ocean, so when I had some time off I'd go down and throw a line in. That seemed to help take my mind off things.

After all, you just had to keep going. Del and I had bought a house we couldn't afford, so I was working two jobs to make ends meet. The financial pressures gave me plenty of other things to worry about. But sometimes, when you least expected it, the memory would pop up in my mind. The brain's funny like that. It seems to catch you off-guard.

I never even spoke to Del about it. I've never been one to wear my heart on my sleeve. I'd never let on that something was wrong. Didn't want to bother her. So I kept it to myself and stewed silently.

Would counselling have helped? I've no idea. Maybe it would. Looking back, I'd say it probably would have been useful. A lot of things have passed through my life, and it probably would have been good to talk about them. Back then, you basically tucked them away in a little box, shut the lid, and hoped you'd never have to open it again.

Talking about this now is like opening the lid of that long-forgotten box.

Having grown up in the country, I was very familiar with death; I had seen animals die horrible deaths from being trapped and poisoned. Even that was no preparation for close encounters with dead human bodies. During my eleven years in the Brigade, I saw five bodies and nothing prepares you for that.

Another strong and sad memory from those years was going to a fire at a function room where a buck's party had been held the night before. We went in and found there were two exits which were both locked—and a dead young man fallen at each locked door trying to escape from the fire. I lost a lot of sleep over that over the years—I had to learn to get

The Frogmore Farmer

on with life and not to let my mind wander back to such dark places.

Manly was my first posting. I was really proud to be told after I started there that the Board of Fire Commissioners, which controlled decisions about appointments and postings, had contacted the College and requested a suitable appointment for Manly. As it turns out, I was the trainee they recommended.

Me in my Fireman's uniform

My first commanding officer was Morrie Stolmac. At that time the Fire Brigade was financed by contributions of three-quarters from the insurers, and one eighth from each of the local and state governments. The union was entitled to have a representative on the Board of Fire Commissioners. Morrie was the union representative on the Board and he was very good to me. I enjoyed my time working with him and I earned a reputation for being committed to my work.

Here's the funny thing about Morrie—he was suave and well-spoken, hardly your typical fireman. He was tallish, about the same height as me, but not one of your beefy types. Morrie didn't swear, smoke or drink, and he never ate meat. Always dressed immaculately. He'd siddle up to you and put his arm around your shoulder. I absolutely bloody detested that. I could feel myself shrinking away. Except for the fact he was married with kids, you'd almost think he was gay.

As the senior fireman at the station, Morrie couldn't afford to take himself seriously. There'd always be someone ready to take him down a peg or two. Maxy Price was one of the tough nuts up at Manly. He sized Morrie up pretty good. He used to say to him, 'All you need is a good root and a feed of steak.' I heard him say that many a time, even though Morrie was in charge. But Morrie just took it on the chin.

I have always worked hard in all of my jobs and have found it to bring its own rewards and satisfaction. I was also fortunate at that posting to be working with a colleague, Les James. Although I could not see it at the time because of my inexperience, Les was a first-rate officer. He was a couple of notches above me in the ranks. He was ex-army, having served in Korea. He was a short little fellow, a bit nuggety, and as blonde as blonde can be. Les was a straight-down-the line sort of guy. None of Morrie's cuddly shenanigans. He was married to a blonde named Beryl, and they had this little tribe of blonde children.

Les's nickname was 'Billy Graham', because he was into religion. Didn't drink, didn't smoke. He went to church all the time. Mind you, he used to change religions like he changed cars. I don't take any notice of that. It's as though he was searching for something he was never going to find. To me, religion divides people rather than bringing them together. Del recently caught up with an old friend. They fell out forty years ago, and that was over religion.

Anyway, Les was the sort of bloke who'd do anything to help you. He took me under his wing and sat me down with an exercise book in which I dutifully recorded his *dos and don'ts*, which became an invaluable way of learning for me. This was important, because we were always doing exams. They were how you won promotions in the Fire Brigade—

by passing your exams. There was an exam after six months, twelve months, two years. The results went to Morrie, who had the power to say *yes* or *no.*

Sometimes I wished he wasn't so helpful. One area where Les wasn't as talented as he thought was in the area of motor mechanics. I had this little Vanguard, and even though it was new the engine had a miss. In those days you hardly got any warranty with a new car. Pretty obvious why, when you look back. Anyway, Les reckoned the valves needed grinding, so he had a go at it. Two days later the car's still not running right, because he'd stuffed up the timing.

After he's finished fiddling with the motor he goes to put the spark plug leads back on. I said to him, 'Les, I think the plug leads should go there and there.'

He said, 'No, I'm sure I've got it right.'

Beryl said, 'Can't you listen to what Brian is saying?'

But Les wasn't having any of that. He put the plugs and wires in his way, hit the starter, and *poof*! It all went up in a puff of blue smoke.

He stared at the engine and said, 'Well I'll be blowed!'

We did some small building jobs together on the side, and Del and I would go on picnics with him and Beryl and the kids. One time before any of us had kids we went to the Rocklily restaurant at Mona Vale.

Les and I remained firm friends until his death in 2013.

Phil Dryden was another fireman who became a good mate. Our kids grew up with his kids. We had picnics with his family during our time off, and we had a gardening job together. Actually, Phil started me in the lawn mowing business when he got me a job up top of Manly—one-and-a-half acres, which is a decent sort of spread.

There were a few other characters in the Fire Brigade.

One bloke had been a boxer before he joined. He'd fought at the stadium in Rushcutter's Bay a few times. Maxy Price called him Canvas—as in he was always on the canvas after being knocked out.

Then there was Jimmy Miles. Another officer was having trouble getting his wife pregnant, and was foolish enough to tell Jimmy his problems. Well, Jimmy was nothing if not caring. He said to this bloke, 'The best thing you can do for your wife is go home tonight, put her in a hot shower, as hot as she can stand. Then put her on the bed, lay her down, get some talcum powder and sprinkle it all over her. Rub it around everywhere, and then ring me—we'll get her pregnant.'

You'd think he'd get his head knocked off—but people took that sort of ribbing. I never indulged in it myself. I don't like it, so I laid off it. As I result, I didn't have those kinds of insults thrown back at me.

The Fire Brigade work required a tremendous amount of maths—calculating heights and pressures etc. were daily tasks. Even though my schooling had been so erratic, I had my basic maths and was good at it. So after being accepted as a probationary fireman for a year, I learned on the job and at college in Sydney. I got into the Brigade because I had a cousin in the Brigade (whose prospective father-in-law was an Officer-in-Charge at the time) and he loved it and kept encouraging me to apply. In about 1958 I threw my hat into the ring and was accepted.

In our training we trained in physical fitness, rope climbing, ladder climbing (at great heights), and pump work. There was also the Smoke Room exercise. This exercise, in which our performance was assessed, required us to enter a completely dark smoke filled room, try to locate a "body" and retrieve it. We had to hold our breath and get in and out as quickly as possible—seconds. I soaked a handkerchief, stuffed it in my mouth and held my breath. The smoke inevitably affected our lungs and eyes and the coughing and spluttering started. My eyes ran for days after those exercises.

I found the physical training demanding at first but just kept at it, and found that it became easier with practice and as my skills and confidence developed.

Not all the probationary firemen made it through—we had to also do drills where we arrived at a location, all the fireman dismounted and the Officer in Charge shouted directions as to the task each fireman was to do. The drills were never what we were to do at a real fire but were designed to train you to respond to commands quickly and effectively in the heat of the moment and to get the calculations for hose pressure exactly right for the conditions in which you were working. Some of the probationers just could not work under that pressure and left. I enjoyed the problem solving and liked learning the technical skills and a lot of those continued to be relevant to my work even after I left the Brigade in 1969.

The camaraderie of the Brigade was one of the things that kept you there. I trained and worked with some real villains. While we were at College I drove my car in each day. Early in my training I finished for the day and returned to my car to find that some larrikins had formed a team, physically lifted up the car, turned it parallel with the road and delicately placed it between two buildings with only inches between the front and rear of my car and the buildings! I was stuck—I couldn't drive forwards, or backwards and they had all stayed behind, in hiding, to laugh as the full extent of my predicament dawned on me.

Of course, the only solution was to lift the car back out,

and they stuck around to help me out, thankfully. I had a good laugh with them at the time but I do not see myself as a prankster—I prefer not to call people by names (e.g. English people "poms")—I always felt there was something disrespectful and sometimes cruel in name calling so I chose to avoid it. I also avoided participating in some of the so-called initiation rites prevalent at that time as I believe it is cruel to humiliate people. There is always an exception to the rule, however, and I well recall a prank of which I heartily approved.

One of the trainees was always causing trouble—he'd swing the rope while someone was climbing it, and he was notorious for asking the instructor, right at the end of the day, a question which inevitably required a fifteen-minute answer. He was just one of those arrogant little pricks who pisses everyone off.

On the day we were passing out from college, a couple of the hard men in our group waited until everyone was dressed in our street clothes, ready to head out to our designated stations. They grabbed the troublemaker, held him down, stripped the lower half of his body and generously applied black boot polish (allegedly supplied by the Brigade) to his genitals!

We had these big tins of boot polish and the Brigade expected us to polish every bit of leather until it gleamed. Well, they gave this little bastard the full treatment. I never saw this—I only heard about it later. I was pleased they got him, because with all the trouble he caused, he more than deserved it.

Whether you made friends or enemies during training, you were unlikely to see many of them again. You might be sent to any one of 33 fire stations, and each station had four shifts with ten firemen per shift. Not to worry—as I soon discovered, you made new friends pretty quickly once you were assigned to your station, and your shift.

Tom Flanagan & me at Narrabeen Fire Station.

Another thing you learned as a fireman was about being a team player—our lives depended on each other out on the job. You had no choice, really. I went to a fire in Manly with a young fellow called Jimmy. I'd swapped shifts from A Platoon to B Platoon, and Jimmy was in B Platoon. The place was well alight when we arrived, so we got the ladder up the side of it. Well, Jimmy wanted to be the hero. He grabbed the hose and up the ladder he went. I was behind him lightening up the hose. You want to take the pressure off the bloke with the nozzle.

Jimmy was supposed to get the water on the fire, but instead he went to water himself. He started to panic. He said, 'Don't you leave me, Brian.'

I said, 'I'm not going to bloody well leave you.' We're both up the ladder, the roof's burning, it's not a picnic. Somehow he pulled himself together and we got through it. Afterwards, he was fine. Mind you, we never talked about it.

Another time, I attended a fire at a school with two other officers. The first officer was on the pump that night and the hose was two and three-quarter inches but the pump operator got the pressure wrong and we could not hold the hose—it was out of our control, twisting and turning and throwing us around like an angry python, and could have killed us. I said to the other officer 'I'll fall on this hose to try to control it, you go and tell that bloke to get his pressure right'. So I squatted down and jammed the hose with my knee controlling it while they got the pressure right. That error could have cost a fireman (like me) his life. The job required us to calculate the pressure at the pump and in relation to the height of the nozzle and he had clearly miscalculated.

If you disagreed with an Officer in Charge at a job, you could not say a word—it was our job to do exactly as he said. There was one job at Civic in Canberra where we were called to an old unoccupied police station which was an L-shaped building. Our officer took us through the building which was really dangerous—burning timber falling down all around us, smoke blinding us. We were obliged to follow him but he put us in a dangerous situation—there should have been an attack on the fire instead of leading the men through the building.

I also remember going to a fire late one night with my colleague Megsy Kirkwood, a red-headed tough man with a nose that looked like he ran into parked cars in his spare time. The fire was at Curl Curl tip in the middle of a violent electrical storm with lightning striking the ground all around us. As it was a tip fire, and contained, it was safe to let it burn itself out. There we stood, out in the open, with brass buttons all down our jackets, steel axes and a metal spanner hanging from our belts, and our enormous brass helmets on our heads. It was horrific. I was terrified we would be struck

The Frogmore Farmer

by lightning and suggested that we at least return to the engine for safety—he would have none of that! Megsy was a real character—he played rugby league until he turned forty and would do anything for you. He regularly shared the fruits of his fishing and crabbing expeditions with our family. His preferred fishing bait was half a plug of gelignite in a bottle!

That's a true story. God knows where he got the idea from. His fishing mate was a copper, so you can use your imagination. I never went fishing with him—I wouldn't be game. Fishing's one thing. Blowing up the Narrabeen Lakes is something completely different.

That's where Megsy went fishing, in Deep Creek. It's a tributary to the Lakes. It's where they made the television series *Whiplash*, about the history of Cobb and Co. They wouldn't have wanted Megsy and his gelignite going off while they were filming.

Myself, I don't know the first thing about fishing. Sure, I'd throw a line into the ocean near the fire station, but that was just to relax. I never expected to catch anything.

One time I caught a fish—a baby shark, by the look of it—and a knapsack full of beer. The shark was maybe two feet long. I didn't know what to do with it so I threw it on the vacant lot next door. Richard still has that knapsack. When I told Megsy the next day he asked me what kind of fish it was.

'Buggered if I know,' I said. 'Looked like a baby shark to me.'

I could see he didn't believe me. Being a keen fisherman Megsy had a fishing book in his locker. He went and got it and started flicking through the pages.

'There is it,' I said. 'A baby shark.'

'You stupid bastard,' he said. 'That's not a shark. That's a flathead. A beautiful-sized flathead. What did you do with it?'

I had to confess that I'd dumped it.

'You stupid bastard!' he said.

I was never a keen fisherman. I got bored too quick. One time though my next door neighbour—Harman Van der Zar was his name—asked me to go down to the lake with him to fish by the bridge. I took a bag of burley and kept throwing it into the water while Herman ripped those fish out with his line. We ended up with three or four kilos of fish—a decent-sized bagful. We went fifty/fifty on those. That was the only time I enjoyed fishing, although I was just the burley thrower. Harman was the one reeling them in.

Dad and I went trout fishing when I was a kid. We'd follow the rapids up and down the river. He used a fly, or just a float and lure. Dad loved it. We'd walk for miles, and Mum would drive the ute down to the crossing at a place called Taralga, behind Goulburn, and wait for us. If we caught fish we'd have lunch. If we didn't, we'd go without. Simple as that.

Mind you, Dad usually caught something. I was just the whipping boy, carrying all the gear and satisfying his need for a fishing trip. I never had the patience for fishing. I'd rather be riding horse or shooting rabbits—keeping on the move. But Megsy and his gelignite would have been too much excitement for me.

On one occasion Megsy accompanied me in my second job. At the time I was working for a lady at Terry Hills who had a small acreage and I assisted her by fencing, rotary hoeing paddocks and planting for her to grow food and generally doing around the property what she required. On the day I refer to, she had asked me to attend to the slaughter of her pig, Melissa, which had been reared by her. Megsy came to assist, along with another fireman friend, Norm. Megsy brought with him his trusty revolver that held .22 short bullets. We had moved Melissa into the yard and Megsy fired but just at the crucial moment Melissa moved her head and the bullet creased her head and sent her into a frenzy. She smashed her way out of the yard with the three of us in hot pursuit across hill and down dale. Ultimately we did the deed, but, as was often the case where Megsy was involved, not as originally planned.

During my service with the Brigade I was posted at Manly, Crow's Nest, Castlereagh Street, Dee Why, Narrabeen, and Civic after that I transferred to Canberra. At that time, in one twenty-four-hour period there were four shifts—one off work and the others all working an eight-hour shift. We slept during our shift at the station between call outs. I hated trying to sleep during night shift at Narrabeen because the noises of the lapping ocean waves kept me awake!

During my years with the Brigade, we were a busy family. As usual, I was working two jobs, the Brigade and the lawn mowing business until I sold the mowing business and worked as a builder with my friend Morrie.

One of my second jobs could have brought my fire brigade career to an abrupt halt. With a few of my colleagues I had taken a job to clear some scrub and we had stacked up winrows of scrub and could not decide how to dispose of the cleared trees and branches. It occurred to us that burning it was the solution. We lit a fire and, without warning, a strong wind came up and suddenly the fire was out of control. We had to call the Brigade! Unfortunately, the Sydney Morning Herald published a photograph of me, in civilian clothes, bravely working alongside the Fire Brigade officers fighting the fire—fortunately nobody knew I had lit the fire! I had to invest in a carton of beer for my colleagues to keep that quiet.

Through those years, Del was also working hard. When we met she was completing her apprenticeship in Crookwell as a switchboard operator. The girls on the switchboard learned from the calls that various callers wanted to place bets with off-course (illegal) bookmakers and also learned the identity of the local bookmakers willing to take those bets. The girls were able to connect callers seeking a bookmaker with the bookmakers and were duly rewarded with boxes of chocolates—the size of the box of chocolates was directly proportionate to the size of the win!

After our marriage in 1956 until 1959 Del worked operating the switchboard at the Melbourne Steamship Company. She then obtained work closer to Manly at a job installing elements into toasters until Diane was born. After the children were born, Del was busy on the home front with the children and running the home. She bore the brunt of our rudimentary housing at Elanora, until I was able to extend the house and make necessary improvements to it. When I think of the modern conveniences we now take for granted compared with our home then, I wonder how she managed.

After we moved to Canberra, Del worked in

Del worked on the switchboard at the Government Printing Office for 18 years.

childminding, then as a white-gloved coin inspector of the Mint Proof Coin Sets at the Royal Australian Mint, and then was appointed to a temporary position as a switchboard operator at the Australian Government Printer, where she stayed for the next eighteen years!

Let me take you on a tour of the Elanora house as it was when we first moved in...

CHAPTER FOURTEEN

Elanora Heights

When we started renting it from relatives of Del's, the home was a small two-bedroom home, with a lounge, kitchen, laundry, and bathroom. There was a small lean to carport but I took that down after we became the owners. Within about eighteen months of moving in, they offered us the chance to buy the place which we did, going into serious debt to do so. We only sold it to move to Canberra.

When we moved in, there was no plumbing into the house, no functioning chip heater– we brought water in from the water tank. You had to boil the water in the copper in the laundry and carry it through the house to the bath—there was no shower. We did have power and after some years installed a telephone. Eventually we had water plumbed into the house.

Our first home at 9 Iluka Avenue, Elanora Heights.

Of course there was no sewerage and the ground was hard and rocky which precluded the installation of septic systems. Until we sold the home, the sewerage was collected by the nightsoil carter whose job it was to come in to the external earth closet, remove the can full of excrement and run back with it to the collecting truck then return the empty can to the closet, a most unpleasant job!

There was one particular occasion when we knew the can was full and for a bit of sport Del and I watched the night carter come in and grab the can and hoist it up onto his shoulder. He promptly spilled the contents over his shoulder and down his back! He got down to the truck and tipped it in, then we watched in horror as he pulled off his little beret and mopped at his shirt—then put the beret back on his head! What a job! They deserved every bottle of beer we gave them at Christmas.

I tried to avoid leaving them a full can especially when we had had visitors by taking the can and climbing through the wire dividing fence to the vacant land next door where I buried the nightsoil but I had to dig a trench because the ground was too hard to dig to any depth.

Although the house was basic, as were most houses at that time, it was in a beautiful location. We enjoyed an easterly aspect and were one mile from the beach on an elevated block with beautiful ocean views. It was a great environment for the children and over the years we extended the house by adding rooms and improved it. The house had Cyprus pine polished floors which Del polished to a high shine with beeswax and brown boot polish.

I'd get the beeswax from the fire brigade. Beeswax was part of our supplies and like any government department they'd often over-stock. So the Commanding Officer would,

'If you want some beeswax take one of those tins.' He was just happy to clear it out of the storeroom. We couldn't afford to have out floors polished professionally, so I was happy with the hand-me-downs. When you mixed the polish and the beeswax you came up with the light brown colour which gave a beautiful shine to the floors. You could see your face reflected in the timber when you lay down. And if you scuffed it, no problem. It'd polish out in a jiffy. The year before we left that house we put carpet down, but I still love the look and smell of timber floors.

Sometimes I'd be so tired from working I'd lie down on my back on the floor and flake out for twenty or thirty minutes.

My sister has a farm at Murrumbateman, between Canberra and Yass. I gave the polisher to her when we were done, and she still uses it. She uses it for the tiles on her patio. Fifty-nine years later and that polisher is still going strong!

It saddens me now to think of the sacrifices Del made over those years. When we had dinner she'd give me the steak, while she ate the lamb chop. Back then lamb chops were dirt cheap. Del told me she didn't like steak. But she's told me since that wasn't true. She was putting me ahead of herself, and that saddens me. I've done the same for her, but for different reasons. If I'd known how much she was giving up I'd have made the move to Canberra years earlier, but when you had a good job you stuck with it. You didn't just walk away from a permanent job, not with a wife and children to look after.

When I saw a chance to work in Canberra with the fire brigade I applied for the job and I won it. They paid for us to move and gave us a house when we arrived, which was a big part of the deal. Not that the house worked out for us. Del hated the place and wanted to go back to Sydney. She was having nervous problems as a result of her thyroid trouble. There was an old doctor who was supposed to be treating her but he didn't know his stuff. I got stuck into him. I wanted to know why he wasn't treating Del better.

When I was a young bloke we never locked the doors to the house. The people were friendly around where we lived. We used to leave the back door unlocked at Elanora Heights, until someone came in and nicked our camera off the kitchen table. That opened our eyes, coming from a community like Boorowa. You realised it can be a silly thing to do, trusting people.

When I think back on those years, it was struggle street for us, but we were happy. I was only twenty-four when Diane, our first daughter, arrived in July 1959. I was both excited and scared. We had a big mortgage, and now Del wasn't working. This was the start of some of the hardest years of my life.

We devised our own budgeting system of putting money aside into different jars to pay the milkman, baker, butcher etcetera. I was still a smoker and Del had her weekly visit to the hairdresser.

After Christine was born in 1962, I built two rooms onto the house, doing all the labour in my spare time and using second-hand bricks.

Diane was born in 1959, Christine in 1962 and Richard in 1964—all came home to that house. Del and her mother sewed clothes for the children and always had them well presented. At that time, I was a member of the Manly-Warringah Football Club and I went to the Club and put three two shilling coins into the poker machines and won enough to buy the children new shoes. I knew to quit once I had won, the machines always win in the long run if you keep playing.

Through those years, I feel now that I walked around half asleep most of the time as I was working two jobs—at the Brigade and in the building business. Del looked after me, making sure I got the steak while her meal was more modest. When I think back now on that time, it saddens me to think of the sacrifices she made, and I am grateful to her for making them with no fuss or fanfare.

Me & Diane building some walls at the Elanora house.

Although I enjoyed my work at the fire brigade, the pay was not good and the shift work system enabled most of us to take a second job to supplement our income. When we moved to Canberra in the late 1960's, I made the same pay from one day building as I made from a week's work at the Brigade.

My first 'second' job was my mowing business which worked by word of mouth. It was very efficient as at one time I had five people in the same street. They each very kindly plied me with cups of tea and cakes and I had to discreetly find ways of disposing of the food when they were not looking—they were killing me with kindness! I worked the run up and sold it to another fireman after about a year.

I had met my friend Morrie by then. His real name was Morris Montgomery and I started out working for him. Morrie and his wife became dear friends to Del and me. There is a story behind how I started working for Morrie—an example of the old saying 'it is not what you know but who you know'. I was doing a gardening job for Morrie's mother in law, not knowing Morrie was her son-in-law, when she asked me to remove a privet hedge. Privet hedges are dense scrubby, difficult things to remove and it was not an easy job but I duly removed it. Unbeknown to me, Morrie had previously attempted to get rid of it and he was a big strapping man but had given up on it. When he next visited his mother in-law and saw the hedge gone, he made enquiries as to how and by whom it had been removed. Soon afterwards I had a call from Morrie offering me work. We did not know each other at all and he asked if I knew carpentry work as well as garden work and after I confirmed I did, I started working for him on a part time basis and that continued for ten years.

Morrie was an unusual man. For him, I did carpentry work, worked as a stonemason and built sea walls—anything he needed. He would buy blocks of land that the developers couldn't sell to anyone else, because they were so hard to build on. Two sites really stick in my mind. One was on the waterfront at Seaforth. Morrie had to build a sea wall first, then steel beams to sit the house on. By building the sea wall he also gave himself a larger area of land to build upon! After that, we had to construct stone steps back up the cliff, which was how I learned stonemasonry.

There was another block in Avalon that was so steep we slid the timber from the road down the slope to a little plateau. It probably destroyed some native habitats on the way through! Then you'd have to go down and unravel the timber. We built a three-storey house on a block that most people would have thought was only suitable for mountain goats.

He was a big man, thick-set, not fat but well-muscled. Six foot one or two, broad shouldered, with very thick wavy hair. He combed it up in front so he looked like he was in the army. Mind you, he never looked aggressive. You'd call him a gentle giant.

He made money from his building. Where he lived would be worth a fortune now. Just across the road overlooking the water. His wife still lives there.

I was as strong as Morrie and the other fellows. I matched it with them, and that's why I've got a bad back now. A lot of the work I've done has been hard on my back—shearing when I was sixteen or seventeen, bricklaying and as a builder.

As a young bloke I worked on the farm next door to Fern Hill, carting bales of hay. There was one fellow there, ex-army, in his thirties, a big strong bullocking sort of bloke. We were having lunch as he was giving exhibitions of how to disarm people. He grabbed me and bent me over backwards. Disarm me? I couldn't bloody move. That's when I first felt my back go.

I yelled out 'You rotten bastard,' but I didn't swear. It was a very religious household, so you watched your tongue.

I reckon I slipped a disk or something. I had a sore back for weeks. But I wasn't going to let on. You didn't show any sign of weakness. So I wasn't going to let him know he'd hurt me.

These days you see guys at weddings and funerals sitting there sniffling. Back then if you cried, you were a wuss. You didn't react. But now I see the stupidity of trying to cover up your feelings. Mind you, I didn't realise this until I was 65, maybe 70 years old. So I must be a slow learner.

The work I did with him gave me the confidence to take on work when I moved to Canberra that no one else wanted because the jobs were out of the ordinary. For instance, when Richard was my apprentice we worked on a home on a slope excavating underneath the existing footings and, using a quick setting concrete, we did quite a large extension working our way down the block and under the existing construction, creating the footings as we went.

Del and I worked out very early that she loved attending to the 'inside' work at the home and looking after the children, and I was good at addressing the 'outside' work and 'bringing home the bacon' as the saying goes. We agreed the children would be raised as Methodists and she took them to Sunday school each week when they were younger.

As a father, I really wanted to give our children happy childhoods—my own childhood held a lot of sadness, mainly because of my father's alcoholism and the shame he brought on our family through that addiction, which none of us understood at that time. I firmly believe that children all need love and protection and I took my responsibility to provide that love and protection very seriously.

Dawn

Del had a younger sister Dawn, who is a story in herself. Dawn was epileptic. She was the baby of the family, and quite a bit younger than Del. When she had a turn she'd attack people, both physically and mentally. She'd attack her mother. Her grandmother came to stay when Dawn was nine, and she put her out of the house. She would become very aggressive.

Dels' brother Barry owned the farm next door. He was next in line after Del. When Dawn went off the rails Barry would come down and give her a good smacking, to bring her down to earth. Ross, the other brother, could do the same, but he got cruel with her.

Dawn actually got married when she was about twenty-five. Del was concerned—she thought it was ridiculous, and tried to stop the wedding. The minister rang her up and told her there was no way of stopping it. Dawn was marrying this bloke who was strange—he had to be, to marry her. They weren't compatible. But the minister told Del that because they can both sign their names on the wedding certificate, no one could stop them.

So Del organised the wedding for Dawn. It was a beautiful wedding, and we still have photos of it. The bloke she married was mentally retarded. He was a big man, but he'd drive you nuts repeating everything over and over. He might say, 'It's a good day today,' then repeat it over and over. One time Del and I were driving them to Crookwell. He was sitting in the back with Dawn. Every hundred yards he'd say, 'The Canberra races are on today.' We laughed so hard I had to pull over because I couldn't drive the car. I'm not a giggler, but that cracked me up.

Dawn's epilepsy affected her badly. They took her to Sydney and operated on her. The doctors took out half her brain—the dead side of her brain. If someone had a go at her, she'd say to them, 'I've only got half a brain—what's your excuse?' You had to laugh with them.

We spent a lot of time with Dawn. When Del's mum died, they moved Dawn to a home in Canberra where they looked after people with those problems. It was run like a boarding house. She was there for a good number of years. Then Dawn and her husband moved into a rental place in Crookwell—that was her downfall. Del's father said he'd like her to come,

Family photo taken at Diane's wedding. Me, Ena, Dawn, Les, Del, Flo & Ross.

but Dawn's husband drove everyone nuts at the church because he spent all his time there. When church was on he wanted to be part of the service.

Del's father spoke to me about it. He said, 'What do you reckon I should do about Dawn? I've got four kids and only three are normal. I'm worried if anything happens to me.'

I suggested he leave the house at Crookwell as a home for Dawn, as long as she needed it. He wasn't sure. I said, 'go and talk to your solicitor. See what he advises.' I'd had experience with this before, that's how I knew about it.

So Dawn and her husband lived in the Crookwell house after Del's father moved into a Salvation Army home in Goulburn. The house passed on to his the four children—they had equal shares—but Dawn could live there as long as she wanted. Once she moved out the place would be sold. Barry was OK with this, but Ross would have rather sold the house. Del and Barry clubbed together and outvoted him.

I always reckoned that once Dawn moved out, the dust won't be settled on the road before Ross had it on the market. Eventually, they moved Dawn to a special needs home in Goulburn. Dawn and her husband had broken up by this stage. She had her own flat, a lovely little bed sitter with its own kitchen, laundry and lounge. We chipped in and bought new furniture for her. Her flat was attached to the main area, where there were people who could look after her.

From where I see it, Dawn had an excellent life. The people around her might have been miserable, but she was good. She was well looked after, no doubt about that. We were involved when she lived at the rented house in Crookwell, and very much involved when she lived in the family house after Del's father moved out. It was a lot harder on Del than me. I was just the back-up. We helped each other out—that's the way it's been all through our marriage. A lot of people don't understand. They say you need to have your own life, but our life is one another. Dawn's been dead for eight years now.

Barry was alright, as long as he didn't have any whiskey in him. He was a bad bloke once he got on the drink. A bloody smooth character, he played tennis, and loved his hair. He thought his hair was fantastic, which it was. The whole family had beautiful thick hair.

To be honest I used to have pretty good hair myself. One time when Del was in hospital, her mother came to stay with us to help look after the kids. We were washing up one night and she said, 'It's no damned wonder your kids have got beautiful heads of hair. Del's is absolutely magnificent and yours is fantastic.' I couldn't believe my mother-in-law was saying this about me! I used to have thick wavy hair but I've got none now.

Brian Dromgold

Spit and Polish

During my eleven years with the Fire Brigade in Sydney, I served at Dee Why the longest. It was the central station on the Northern Beaches, the lynchpin if you like. We had lots of calls out to bushfires, as well as house fires.

One thing that annoyed me about the fire brigade was their emphasis on spit and polish. They had you polishing and polishing to keep you out of trouble on the day shift. As blokes moved up the ranks their power would go to their heads. Just say you'd worked at a station with a bloke for five years, off and on. He'd become an officer and come back and start dictating his requirements to his team. A lot of the blokes would just laugh at him. They were hardened fellows, ex-wharfies and ex-miners.

Sometimes they'd laugh at him behind his back, then do what he wanted. Other times, they'd have something over him. One bloke worked as a cabbie on his days off, which was totally illegal. He came back as an officer—still working as a cabbie, mind you—and started throwing his weight around. So someone threatened to dob him in. 'Keep up this shit and I'll let the higher-ups know you've been driving a cab for years.' Well, that sat him back on his arse, let me tell you. He didn't want to lose his job, so he cut the crap from that moment on.

Keeping your commanding officer under control counted for nothing if they sprung a surprise inspection on you. We had these old Dennis fire engines, the classic English models with no roof, a solid brass radiator, and mudguards the size of a spinnaker on those big racing yachts. When you were called out to a fire you'd have three firemen sitting on each side, facing outwards, with the driver and station officer up front. They might have looked impressive, but they were a devil to keep clean. Not just clean, but immaculate.

Here's how it worked. An inspector could arrive at any hour, day or night, slip on his white glove, and run it underneath the mudguard. If he found even the merest speck of dirt, you were in deep doo-doo. You'd have to write a foolscap page report explaining why the mudguard was dirty, and you'd have to make three copies. We had no copiers or even carbon paper, so you had to write your report out three times.

I was a slow writer, so it wasn't something I wanted to be saddled with. At this point you'd pass the buck. 'I only came in at 11.00 pm sir, the previous shift must have been too busy after the fire this afternoon up at Collaroy sir, yes sir no sir three bags full sir.' But you'd probably end up having to write that damned report.

As a result of all this hoo-ha we ended up making some silly decisions. If you were called out to a bushfire you'd end up with the Dennis covered with dust and mud. We had these old Blitz trucks that carried thousands of gallons of water. They were mongrels to drive, but you'd rather take them to a bushfire than the Dennis. You'd be thinking about how you're going to clean the damn fire truck when you should have been thinking about putting out the fire!

One time Les and I went out to a fire in the hills up behind Dee Why. Just the two of us—he was the Senior Officer, I was a Fireman First Class. We had to use the Dennis to get the water going. Les manned the pump while I held the hose, because I was the junior.

We put the fire out no problem, but when we got back to the station it was all hands on deck to clean the appliance. None of this sitting in the mess room drinking coffee! Cleaning the engine took hours upon hours. All the couplings and fittings were brass, so you'd have to pull them apart and polish them. The hoses were canvas, so you'd lay them flat and scrub them clean with water and a hand broom, before hanging them on the gantry to dry. No whitener or bleach—just elbow grease. When they had dried you'd roll them up and put them back on the engine. You put the spare hoses on in the meantime.

When you were washing down the fire engine you'd clean under mudguards with brush and hose. When they dried you'd get a chamois and clean under mudguards, then wipe it down completely with a dry cloth to finish the job. That way if the inspector did run his finger underneath he'd find nothing.

You didn't worry if it was too hot or too cold, or if you were knackered from putting out a fire. It was part of the job, so you got it done.

Mind you, it wasn't as frustrating as I've made it sound. I've always been a bit of a clean fiend. I washed my own car and cleaned the wheels. However, I drew the line at cleaning underneath the mudguards!

After eleven years in Sydney it was time to move on. I had a chance to move to Canberra as a fireman, and open a new chapter in our lives.

CHAPTER FIFTEEN

Moving to Canberra

The terms of Uncle John's will were simple. My parents had the use of the farm at Fern Hill while they were alive, after which it passed on to me. I knew that there was an adjoining 700-acre property with valuable standing timber, so I decided that Del and I should move to Canberra. There were jobs going begging in the Fire Brigade in the nation's capital. I would use the sale proceeds of the house in Elanora Heights to buy the 700 acres. During my time off, I could drive up from Canberra, harvest and sell the timber, and make my fortune.

Winning the job in Canberra was easy enough. I was one of five firemen transferred to Canberra. There was one bloke as the Station Officer, while I was given the job of Senior Firemen, which meant I was second in charge at the station. The other blokes filled the remaining positions.

Unfortunately, my grand plan dissolved when we got to Canberra to our rented home organised by the Fire Brigade. I'd been told we'd be given a new house. Yes, we'd be paying rent, but it was only a nominal amount. So we'd be able to sell the house in Sydney and buy the block of land next to the farm at Boorowa. It turned out the youngest bloke got the best house of the lot. Given the troubles Del and I experienced, I found that really galling.

The house they gave us in Dickson wasn't new. It was an

older place that had been freshly painted. All good, except in the kitchen the fat was dripping from the ceiling. The previous tenants had been cooking and cooking and cooking, and the painters hadn't bothered to clean the fat off the walls and the ceiling. They just painted over it. That's just one example; overall, the house was of an extremely poor standard. The kids hated the joint. I remember Christine kicking the wall, she was that angry. But the worst was yet to come, and it hit Del the hardest.

At first, I thought she was just depressed. She'd be up cleaning the spots off the walls at two or three or four o'clock in the morning. Del hadn't wanted to move to Canberra. That was one of the few differences in life we had. Even though we only had a very modest house at Elanora Heights, she didn't want to leave Sydney.

We didn't fight over it. I just told her that I couldn't take it any longer—all the pressure I was under. Moving to Canberra was a chance to change our fortunes. But it didn't work out at first, and that made things worse for Del.

When I started building I'd be working with a mate framing a house, and Del would come and sit outside the job crying. 'Jesus,' I thought, 'this isn't good.' Del went to a doctor who was hopeless. The more he kept treating her the worse she got. He sent her to a psychiatrist who to his credit sent her back to the doctor. The psychiatrist said there was nothing wrong with her, that the problem was chemical.

Well I was so fed up I went in and saw the doctor. I got stuck into him. I said, 'What's going on? You've been treating Del for a year and you haven't found what's wrong with her!'

A couple of days later Del went to him bathed in sweat. It was a cold winter's day, and he asked if she was always this hot. She said 'No, I'm mostly cold.' So he sent her for a final test and BINGO! They diagnosed a thyroid problem. When your thyroid's not working properly it affects your nervous system. They reckon Del had it before she came to Canberra but being in Canberra made it worse.

It turns out Canberra is well-known for thyroid problems. We didn't know it before we moved but we soon learned about it with Del being ill. Canberra's part of what's called a thyroid belt. I don't know the ins and outs of it. Maybe it's the minerals or lack of minerals in the ground. Whatever the cause, Canberra seems to attract thyroid problems the way our property at Boorowa attracted lightning.

There was a fair bit of ironstone in the ground at Boorowa, so when the thunderstorms came that's where the lightning struck. We had trees blown up—huge gum trees. They'd splinter into pieces the size of wooden fence posts. Imagine that. They were good for firewood because they were dead the moment they hit the ground.

Our house was struck a couple of times, too. You could see the marks on the weatherboards where the lightning had scorched them. Once, in the middle of a massive thunderstorm, the roof lifted slightly. We were inside trembling with fear. Fortunately, the roof settled back in the right place.

So when I think of Del's depression and her thyroid problems, I think of those big storms at Boorowa. If you're living someplace you have to deal with whatever cards you're dealt. We're just lucky that after Del's operation everything settled back in the right place—just like the roof on our house in Boorowa.

Not that the operation was easy. The doctors told me they'd have to cut Del's throat. Back when I was working as a rouseabout I'd slaughter and skin four sheep each evening to feed the shearers. How did I slaughter them? By cutting their throats. I'd seen what happened to sheep once you cut their throats, so I couldn't figure how Del would survive.

I had nightmares about it. Real nightmares. My farm experience taught me the seriousness of the operation. I was worried she wouldn't survive, I thought it would be touch and go. I never spoke to Del about my fears because I didn't want to worry her, but I spoke to her Mum and Dad. They came over from Crookwell and sat there with me at the hospital while we were waiting for it to happen. The doctors didn't even explain it. These days they draw a sketch and explain the procedure, so you're more at relaxed about it all. But I had terrific fears, and the doctors did nothing to set my mind at ease.

The operation only took an hour, and it turned out to be not such a big deal at all. They cut around a crease in her neck, and now you can't even see a scar. They took out two-thirds of Del's thyroid, and you'd never know they'd been there. Del doesn't even take thyroxin, so they did a bloody good job of it.

When the doctors came out and said she was OK I was elated! We were a pretty strong partnership then—and we still are! I probably had a tear then. I certainly have a tear in my eye now remembering it.

To make matters worse, our sale of Elanora fell through at the last minute, and I was still liable for the rent on the unliveable house. So off I went to grovel in front of the bank manager. At least in those days you could talk to the man who was holding on your fate in his hands. I explained our situation to him and lucky for us he turned out to be a decent bloke.

Part of the problem was the buyer of our Elanora house failing to settle the sale. We'd organized a solicitor to chase up the buyer and force him to come to the party. Because the bank manager knew we were serious about fixing this problem, he went easy on us. He agreed to lend me the money to buy our home at Pearce in Canberra, instead of the 700 acres covered with beautiful millable timber. At the same time, I undertook to pay off the mortgage once the house in Elanora sold.

Financially, it was tough until the sale was completed. We still owed money on the Elanora house, so we had repayments to make. The government insisted that we pay twenty-four weeks' rent on the house they had provided for us. That was ridiculous, because they could have leased the house to someone else straight away, but they had us over a barrel. After all, I was working for them! Plus we had to make payments on the house at Pearce.

At the same time, I made up my mind to keep Del in the manner which she deserved. Every Friday night we'd go out for dinner. No, not fish and chips! I love fish and chips, but you can't get decent fish and chips in Canberra. Just the other night I bought some fish and chips, and they were awful. I couldn't eat them. So nothing much has changed in the last forty years.

No, Del and I would get a takeaway Chinese meal, or go out to a club. Mostly we went to the closest club. It had just opened near our place in Pearce. They were still building it when we joined. Del and I had membership numbers 6024 and 6025. It was a good place to have a meal together on a Friday night. We'd have a meal then head home. Neither of us had any interest in playing the pokies.

Once a month, we'd get together with a group of friends, mostly people we knew from Boorowa who'd moved to Canberra, and go out to one of the top line restaurants. Back then there were twelve quality restaurants in Canberra. Today there'd be a hundred or more. We went around the twelve twice, going from one to the other.

To pay all these bills, I immediately started working a

second job as a carpenter. Bill Allan was working at the main fire station in Canberra, although he was on a different shift to me. Someone told me he was a carpenter, to I spoke with him on the change of shift. Turned out he wasn't a carpenter but a joiner, and good at his trade. Here's the funny thing. He could build cabinets and do all of that intricate finishing work, but he didn't really know how to build a house. I used to joke that I'd take an adze and square off the logs while Bill was doing his fancy cabinet work!

We made a good partnership. We started D & A Builders. Dromgold and Allan. Later on we became Belmont Constructions, inspired by the Holden Belmont. We got a couple of accounts with suppliers to pick up the materials we needed, until we got paid. Money was tight back then. Bill and I joined up with a third bloke, Don, a fantastic tradesman. He was the only bloke I ever knew who could lay out and cut the timber for a roof without looking at a book. He had a real knack for it. He just knew all the angles.

Building a business

The first job we ever did together was not our greatest moment, though. This woman had asked us to build three wardrobes for her. We gave her a quote then realised we'd only priced the materials—we hadn't priced out labour! Well we talked to her and asked if she could come to the party a bit because we were going to be working for nix. She said no. Just as well I was still in the fire brigade with a wage coming in, because those three wardrobes took us a week to build. Jeez, that kicked us—but we never made the same mistake again. Every time we quoted we added labour in first thing.

Everything was go in Canberra in those days. The place

was red hot for builders. So all our money worries were soon settled. I was taking home $28 each week from the fire brigade—that's after tax and ambulance fees had been taken out. Once I'd learned to price my labour, I was making $28 in the hand for each day's work as a builder. How ridiculous is that? Pretty easy to see why I only lasted a year in the fire brigade before going full time as a builder.

$28 may not seem like much, either per day or per week, but you have to remember it was forty-three years ago. Our house in Pearce, a four-bedroom place, only cost us $15,000. So it's all relative.

Here's how Bill and I set up the business. Bill had sold his house in Sydney, so he had some money, which he put into D & A Builders. Don and I paid him interest on this. I mortgaged our house in Pearce as a guarantor for the loans we took out. Don had no money, but plenty of contacts in the finance and building games. So of the three of us, I was the only one in a position to lose everything if we went bust. Bill would lose some money, Don would lose some time, Del and I would lose our home! Fortunately, it never came to that.

Sometimes you just have to live on trust.

Bill was a strong bloke, five foot ten with thick wavy black hair. He loved the grog and he loved women. When his wife went to Sydney to visit his mother he'd get all mockered up in his good cloths and prowl around the clubs. He was a suave looking bloke for sure. Same age as me, but he had a different way of running his life.

Bill spent a lot of time at the Ainslie Football Club. He did however have one big regret in his life. He had a daughter who was fine, and a son who was—I'm not sure how you'd explain it—pretty raucous. The first time Bill and his son came to visit us the son was up on the roof before we knew it. He actually climbed up onto the roof of the house and was walking around up there. There was definitely something wrong with that kid. He didn't comprehend much, his brain just went in swirls. These days you'd probably say he had Attention Deficit Disorder, but it seemed worse than that.

Another time when Bill and I were working on a house out in the bush Bill had a call. Turns out the young bloke had taken Bill's car for a drive. Bill had left the keys at home and that was the only invitation the kid needed. That was Bill's downfall in life. He was so disappointed that he ended up with a child like that. He didn't take it well. I can understand why.

Apart from that he was a cheery bloke. We had all the laughs in the world working together, always cracking jokes and taking the Mickey out of each other. If you're hammering away and you miss the nail he'd say, 'Do you want a bigger bloody hammer with a bigger bloody head?' He wasn't being critical or nasty, just making a comment. Any job I've ever been on you have to do this or you'd go mad. Everyone makes mistakes and everyone jokes around about it. Stops you getting uptight each time you miss that nail.

One of my biggest challenges in the building game was getting a builder's licence. I didn't have any trade qualifications as such. So I had to round up a number of references from people who could vouch for me. Bill had a certificate and he gave me a reference. Don was very competent and well qualified, and he gave me a reference. I also had a reference from Morrie, another from an architect. I presented them all to the building section. They chewed it over and over and decided to grant me a licence. I was thrilled to bits.

I don't know how the building section usually works, so I can't say if this was normal or not. I do know that when Richard went to get his licence they noticed his surname and asked him if Brian Dromgold was his father. When he said that I was they told him I was the only builder they knew in Canberra with a clean record. They had no claims or complaints against my name. I'm not saying I never did anything wrong. I'm saying they didn't see me do anything wrong. Just lucky, I guess.

There's one job Bill and Don and I worked on that really sticks in my mind. It took somewhere between eighteen months and two years, and I went back for many years to finish work. The house was in the bush ten miles out of town. It was designed by Albert Jessie Read, a well-known Canberra architect. Read built his own house down at Lake George out of railway sleepers—that's how nutty he was! Just joking, at least, you might think he was nutty, but he came up with some beautiful designs.

He's designed this house for Peter McCullough, a doctor. He worked at the university and ran his own medical practice once a week. Bill and Don and I had a reputation for building things other builders wouldn't touch. This house was three stories high with steeply pitched roofs. The top story was an attic where Peter was going to have his office. It wasn't a conventional design. The roof was a complex shape, with eight hips coming up to a central stone chimney three stories high. By hips I mean sections of roof that were more or less triangular. They were built with laminated timber beams, and they swooped right down from the peak and dived into the rockwork at ground level. It was more like an igloo than a normal house.

The roof wasn't the only unique feature. The bathtub was in the shape of a coffin, with glass around it so you could see straight in from outside. The chimney wasn't the normal type either; it was more of a u-shape. But the carport really set the house apart. We put in these big fourteen-inch steel beams going across, concrete slabs across that, then tarpaper, then earth. Peter filled it with native plants so when you drove the car down it was like driving underground.

But the roof of the house was Peter's downfall. Inside it was lined with timber, and on the outside it was covered with Western Red Cedar shakes. Timber shingles are cut from a log, so they're more or less uniform. Timber shakes are split from a log so they're rougher—but stronger. They go with the grain.

Anyway, one day Bill and I are up two-thirds of the way up the roof, fitting the shakes. You filled in as you went with the shakes. Peter had the day off from work so he decided to help us lay the shakes. He grabbed a bundle of shakes, hauled himself up the ladder and jumped up on the roof. Did I mention it was really steep? When you climbed the roof you had to put your feet down in a certain way because it was so slippery. Otherwise you'd lose your footing. Peter makes it a couple of metres up the roof when he starts to slip back. The shakes fly out of his hands like a pack of cards and he's backpedalling, backpedalling, then goes arse over and disappears from sight.

Bill and I look at each other. 'Jesus Christ,' Bill says. 'He's dead. Who's going to pay us now?'

Turns out he wasn't dead at all. The roof was so close to the ground he didn't have too far to fall. Maybe seven feet. He grabbed the eaves as he went so his hands were filled with splinters. The gutters were made of cedar too. Just as well—they were strong enough to slow him down, and break his fall.

Don and I built another house for Bert Read up at Molong, northwest of Orange. One of the main ideas was that the place would be built from rocks picked up on the property. My nephew, Christopher, came up with us. It was his job to go around with a tractor and trailer, picking up rocks and bringing them in for the rock hoppers to build walls two stories high. There was even a pool that went into the family room. The water lapped on the bottom of the wall. You could dive into the pool in the family room, swim under the wall, and go outside to swim in the rest of the pool. Well, you could if you wanted to be a silly bugger.

One time Bert Read came up to study the farm for ideas. His wife came up from Canberra with him. She decided to sunbake in the nude, and the next-door farmer came riding over the hill. His horse got a hell of a shock. True story.

One of our first spec homes I built with Bill and Don got knocked back by the authorities because it was too close to the ground. They used to measure them. You had to be twelve inches clear, and we were about a third of an inch short. So what could we do? We couldn't dig it out, so we found a mate with a strong jack, and lifted the house that bit extra. There was always a bright spark in the team to solve problems. The secret is to keep going when you come up against a problem, and work your way around it.

In building, problem solving is absolutely paramount. This is where those skills I learned from early in my life—how to work with my hands, how to fix things, how to solve problems—kicked in.

The three of us also rebuilt an old coach house and blacksmith's shop at Bungendore. It was a two-storey place, built of stone and iron that had existed since the bushranger days. It had been a stopover point for the stage coaches. One wall had a hole in it ten foot by eight, which we had to patch. We cut three new windows and doors, and power cleaned the soot that had built up over many years of blacksmithing from the rafters. Then we lined the rafters to stop any more soot from coming down. We built a mezzanine floor and stairway for the bedroom upstairs. The rooms downstairs, the kitchen, dining and laundry, were quaint but rugged. So I guess you can say we helped preserve a bit of Australia's history.

The building industry has its booms and busts, and around 1977 things tightened up. Bill and Don moved on, and Peter McCullough, the doctor who fell of the roof of his house, recommended me for a job at the Australian National University. Not as a lecturer, surprisingly, but as a carpenter.

Well, after working for myself the money on offer at ANU was pretty lousy. At this time a young builder named John put an ad in the Canberra paper, seeking a building partner. John had subcontracted to Hooker Homes, but his previous partner had moved on.

Del responded to the ad on my behalf, as I was working. John turned out to be twenty-two, twenty years younger than me. He was a wiry young bloke with reddish sort of hair, and very enterprising. I thought we would be mismatched, but we worked together for nearly eight years. It turned out that John had a warped sense of humour, much like mine. Just a little bit off, just a little warped.

One time John and I worked on a mud brick house in the bush. The bricks were straw bales faced with mud from the dam. Our job was to do the timber work. The house had 10 foot ceilings, as opposed to standard 8 foot, so we had problem reaching the ceiling. John and I decided to use our 2 ton trucks as mobile scaffolds. It worked just fine. When John had to get up into the apex of the ceiling, we put the ladder into the tray of the truck. Even though I'd been a fireman, John was the climber. I would stand in the tray, hold on to the ladder, and pray.

Another time John, my son Richard and I were renovating John's in-laws' place. John and Richard were trying to pull

Me & John Moore (taken at my 80th birthday party).

out a corner of a ceiling so they could repair it. The ceiling was fibrous paster, which is much heavier than gyprock.

Suddenly, the entire ceiling gave way, and I wore the whole thing on my head and shoulders. My shoulder was slightly injured, but I was more worried about my head. Luckily, I was wearing a hat. Otherwise, it could have been serious. John just laughed. I was not sure if it was that's funny laugh or that's serious laugh. That was John. A funny bugger.

This reminds me of another story which gives you a sense of John's character. He was working alone, building his own home at Benandarah, down near the south coast. While he was working right up in the roof with a nail-gun, he accidently nailed his hand to the truss. Had to use his hammer to get the nail out. Then he climbed down the ladder to get to his ute, and collapsed. He was half in the ute, half out. When he woke up he could feel the rain dripping on his face. He got himself off to hospital and got patched up. John was tough, and a good mate.

Eventually, John became tired with building, and decided to buy a bobcat. Then he got tired of freezing his arse off in the bobcat in winter, and decided to move down to the south coast.

So then it was just me by myself, until Richard came into the business in 1986. He'd been an apprentice, but came in as a partner once he'd qualified. In 1990, Richard went out building by himself. I worked another ten years before I retired. Well, before I retired officially. I kept working in the trade for many more years, as long as my back could take it.

When Richard was working as my apprentice, we built an extension on a house with a tiled roof. The plan was to take the tiles off the roof, do the extension, then put a corrugated iron roof on it. Removing the tiles was trick because those things were slippery. While we were removing the tiles one of the other apprentices started sliding headfirst down the roof. Luckily, Richard grabbed him by the ankles. When we looked into it we found he'd been smoking wacky baccy. That really opened my eyes. People could turn up for work looking normal, but they weren't.

Some clients I enjoyed working with. Others were less enjoyable. There was one woman who had asked us to build an extension for her. She had gone out to Fyshwick to match her existing tiles. The display board she used to choose her tiles had been up for thirty years, and the tiles had lost all their colour. Needless to say, they didn't match. We went and bought the tiles she'd ordered but when she saw them she refused to pay. I argued and argued with her until I couldn't argue any more. Then Bill said 'Let me have a crack at her.' Well, he must have been a silver-tongued negotiator, because in the end she wanted us to knock five dollars off the bill! The tiles cost several thousand, so why did she waste so much time arguing the point? After all, she was the one who miss-ordered the tiles, not us.

Here are few photos of some of the houses we built during this time.

Whole house built by Belmont Constructions – Jacky Howe Crescent, Canberra.

Half the house cut off and 2 of these extensions added at Yarralumla, ACT.

Whole house built by Belmont Constructions over 18 months at Macks Reef Road, ACT. Stage 1.

Macks Reef Road, ACT. Stage 2. Roof had 8 hips and thousands of shingles.

CHAPTER SIXTEEN

Jack's Funeral

My best friend Jack was a farmer, and he had a fair bit of trouble during his life. After Jack's father died, his older brother Rex left the navy and went to run the farm. Rex shot himself getting through a fence with a .22. When you're fencing if you need to join two strands of number 8 wire you tie them in a bow. As Rex was climbing through the fence the trigger caught in the loop of wire and BANG! He was dead.

I think Rex suffered. He was in the Navy for years. He left a lifetime career, a good paying job, to come out and run the farm. He probably wasn't making any money. He was about sixteen when he went into the navy, so he didn't know anything about farming.

After Rex died, Jack packed in his job working on a farm and went home to stay with his mother, June, and run the family farm. Then she died within a year or two. The family, all six of them kicked up a stink. They wanted to break up the farm—one of the sisters was adamant they had to sell. It was very sad. They got 4,000 quid each, back before decimal currency, so Jack had enough to buy a little place about seven or eight miles out of Boorowa heading to Cowra. Later, his wife Margaret sold it and moved to Canberra and brought a unit here.

In 2006 I was in the middle of cutting in a roof, when I took a phone call from Jack's second oldest son, Ian. Jack was dying of lung cancer, and they wanted me to go and see him in the hospice. The roof was open, rain was coming, and I would have to tarp it before I left. The bloke I was working with was a German bricklayer; he didn't know how to tarp a roof. I told his son I would get over there in two or three hours, but not straight away. I felt bad about it but I couldn't just sit down and bawl my eyes out. I had to get the job done.

All Jack's family were up in Boorowa. The hospice was in Canberra. He had four kids, his wife had relatives. You'd think someone could have popped in to see him, but they had all gone away. As soon as I got off the roof I went around to the hospice. One of his sons had arrived by then, but he'd been alone for two-and a half hours. It took him three more weeks to die. He might have been on his deathbed, but Jack was one tough customer. So I'm glad I got there. I just wish I could have gone straight away.

After that I visited Jack every day until he died. We had fun because I didn't look on him as if he was dying. He just looked like he was going to get better. We relived a lot of old memories. There were a lot of people visiting him. He was a funny bugger—very much unlike me. I'm serious, but he was a funny bugger. He was a great story-teller, a great joke-teller. It wasn't what he said but how he said it. He was bloody dry.

At Jack's funeral I was standing back from the graveside as they were lowering him down the hole. It was a hot day, and they had a canopy over the grave. I was wearing a bushman's hat, a proper one, an Akubra. Jack's widow Margaret spoke to the priest in the middle of the sermon. 'You see that man standing there with the hat?' she said. 'He's Jack's lifelong friend.'

Jack's daughter said the same thing, that I was his best friend.

I overheard then. Only ten feet away. I felt bloody awful, watching my best mate go down. I feel sad thinking about it now.

Here's the eulogy I prepared for Jack's funeral. It's short, but covers a fair bit of ground. This is the first time it's been delivered in public. During the funeral Jack's two sons gave their eulogies. I had hoped to speak at the wake, but the PA system didn't work. There were so many mourners they filled two rooms down at the club. It would not have been possible to deliver a speech to such a large group without the aid of a microphone, so I gave it a miss.

Anyway, here's how I feel about Jack, and how much he matters to me:

Jack was my friend for the past 64 years. That's all bar the first five years of his life.

His life is the stuff of which Australian legends are made. As we were growing up happy and healthy in the Australian bush, we used the open spaces as a playground and the people as teachers and friends.

In the early days our games were those of the innocent adventure of country children. We skinned our knees, burned our faces, and were probably dirty most of the time. Our mothers knew we'd be together and never seemed to worry.

When I think of those days I can remember the feel of the sun and the smell of the country. As we grew so did the adventures. We were really a couple of tearaways getting into mischief and trouble, such as chasing wild horses out of the scrub, cracking whips and getting them caught under the horses' flank, causing them to pigroot or buck. Racing the horses flat-out, strictly forbidden by the families. Borrowing the neighbour's tobacco, which then got washed away. Pinching watermelons or cutting out a deep triangular piece, tasting it, then putting the plug back.

Riding eight miles to the Rugby Show to enter horse events. When a fight started the policeman, Jack Sparks, told everyone to move away from the show and finish their fight, so we rode another eight miles to watch the end. The two fellows had so much skin missing and had knocked over so many saplings that you could really say you'd seen a fight.

Anytime a challenge came up we'd say, 'Have a go and bugger the consequences.' Later going to dances before Del's time at Rye Park, Boorowa, Frogmore, Rugby, Grabben Gullen and Laggan. We were riding motorbikes until we were old enough to get a car licence. It was very often early next morning when we got home and there were often more people came home than went originally.

I remember early one winter's morning this fellow decided to go for a swim in Jack's dam. He stripped down, dived in and came out frozen. He had turned blue and looked like he had two belly buttons—everything else had disappeared.

It was fun. With Jack there was never a dull moment. He was larger than life as a youngster and I guess he remained that way all his life. In my teens I moved away from the farm while Jack stayed to build a life and family. He was my best man at my wedding, and apart from my wife, my best friend throughout life.

We stayed in touch and talked with each other about significant highs and lows as they came along. I knew that each phone call or visit, no matter what the reason, would include a good laugh. Jack often told me how proud he was of his family and how lucky he was. He loved the farm, his family and his life.

It was a really proud moment for both of us earlier this year when at my fiftieth wedding anniversary Jack's grandson and my grandson were both there as friends. We didn't engineer it but it was truly a great thing for us both. We have a great picture of Jack giving a speech, something he was very comfortable doing. I reckon if ever his life story was written it would become an Australian classic—an understated larrikin and a family man, a true blue Aussie with a big heart. John Williamson could have been thinking of Jack when he wrote 'True Blue'.

When I was thinking of what to say today I looked up the definition of true blue. It's a steadfast loyal Australian who displays the Aussie ideals of a fair go for all, mateship and having a go. Says it all I reckon. I'll miss the calls and talks mate, but you'll be with me whenever I think about you.

Even now, when I read through that speech or think of Jack, I have to wipe a tear from my eye.

Jack Elkins at our 50th wedding anniversary in 2006.

CHAPTER SEVENTEEN

Family

By this time, Del and I had three beautiful children. Diane was born in 1959, Christine in 1962 and Richard in 1964. They were great children and have grown into fine adults of whom I am extremely proud. Christine has three children: Kate, Tom and Alice. Richard has four boys: Trevor, Daniel, Jake, and Matthew. Trevor has a son, Seth and Jake has a son Ned. So Del and I are great-grandparents now!

Diane was born with flaming red hair and was a complete charmer—she was a very obedient child and very sweet natured and responsible, although she became a little rebellious as she got older. She was nine when we moved, and the shift to Canberra was hardest on her. She had settled into school in Elanora Heights, where she was top of the class. When she arrived here they put her back a class. Diane bucked and screamed until Del went to see the headmaster and told him it wasn't fair. He gave Diane a test to see how she went, and she was way up there. So they put her up to the next class and she was happy with the win. Diane's just had her 40th reunion with her high school and she had a fantastic time. There were sixty-two former students there; they all came back to Canberra for the occasion.

Christine was the spirited one and spent much of her childhood years running away and escaping! I remember when she was about thirteen we discovered she had been helping herself to my Johnny Walker whisky, replacing it with tea! Christine has a great sense of humour and has us all in fits of laughter as she regales us with her stories.

Richard was four when we arrived at Canberra. He was good growing up. He didn't worry about things like most people do. He'd go off on his bike. Del would say, 'Where are you going, son?' He'd say he was just going for a ride down to the pond. He'd be gone for a couple of hours, and he'd come back with a tin full of tadpoles. Del would tell him to be back in an hour, but Richard and his mate would just disappear. It didn't worry him. He was very casual about things like that.

As he grew up he never changed much. He went on to work with me in the building business. He's very easy going, and doesn't argue at all—he gets that from his mother's side. I think it's great!

P51 - Diane, Christine, me and Richard.

Diane, Christine, Del and Richard.

Richard, Diane & Christine at 2, 9 & 6 years old respectively.

When Christine and Richard were young, I was very impressed by the discipline they displayed by walking the pet dog without being asked. Later we discovered they were meeting their mates at the local school oval and smoking! Of course I had to read the riot act to them about that, notwithstanding the things I did as a youngster!

One thing I noticed about being a parent is that it softens you. Being brought up on a farm, I saw horses as something to ride, cows as something to milk, and calves to slaughter once they were big enough. I used to be able to kill sheep and shoot kangaroos, but I couldn't do it now. Having kids is what changes you.

We lost a cat pretty much the day we moved into Pearce. My cousin came to visit and she ran over it. You know how cats are. They climb up on the wheel to get warm. So I said to the kids, 'Don't worry, pussy's dead, we'll bury it in the backyard and go out and get another pet tomorrow.'

We went and got a white poodle, can you believe it? A little bundle of fluff. I didn't realise you had to shear and clip those things. We had that dog for fifteen years. He was a mid-sized poodle, a great watchdog. He wouldn't let anyone in the back yard if he didn't want them there. The kids saw this white bundle of fluff and fell in love. I was happy for them. All this make you softer.

Another time we visited Dad on the farm. He took the kids cray fishing down at the dam. He caught half a bucketful in twenty minutes. We put a plastic bag over the bucket and brought them back to Canberra. You have to put them in salt water to make them spew and get all the crap out of them. I put them in the laundry tub and they're squealing and carrying on trying to climb up out of the water.

The kids were saying 'Dad, you shouldn't be cruel to them.'

The Frogmore Farmer

Our family. Diane, me, Richard, Del & Christine.

Down by Phil's Creek on our farm at Fern Hill. Me Christine, Richard & Diane.

I said 'No, we're going to cook them.'

They said 'What! How are you going to cook them?'

I said 'You drop them in boiling water.' Well, the shit hit the fan. They wouldn't let me go on with it. I pulled the plug quick, put the crayfish back in the bucket and took them to the Scrivener Dam, which is the main dam that banks up the Molonglo river. I threw them over the side with three kids trailing me. I kept the bucket, and all these crayfish went over the top.

Once Del had the kids settled in school, she worked in the school canteen, where she made a number of friends. She also joined a women's church group, which wasn't as successful. The group was supposed to meet at a different house each week, but they decided that our place was just right for their little ones to wreak havoc. Del complained to me about their behaviour, so I told the church group to shove it, more or

At Elanora. Christine & Diane off to school while Richard pretended.

less. I was nice about it, really, but the group fizzled when they didn't have a house for their little darlings to wreck.

Del gave up church as a result. The other women wanted to go down to the coast and do all sorts of funny things. Del told them she didn't want any part of it. So they came to a parting of the ways.

Canberra was a great place to raise your kids. Richard turned out to be an excellent soccer player and a pretty good cricketer. When he was playing cricket there was no one available to coach his team. So the cricket club asked me to do it. I said, 'I don't know anything about coaching cricket. I don't even like the game. But I'll do it.'

So I front up at the playing fields. You'd never seen such a disaster in all your life. These kids—they didn't tell me to get stuffed to my face—but they might just as well have. One kid wandered off up to the school and started smoking. What do you do? You can't grab the kid by the scruff of the neck and drag him back. The best-behaved kid was Richard. He wasn't game to pull any of those stunts. Not that I think he would have—he was a bit different from the rest. He was more reserved—that is, until he got behind the wheel of a car.

Once I realised I couldn't control the kids, I just walked off and left them. 'If you're not going to do what I you to do want there's no point,' I said. So I went home. Our house was only four houses away from the oval. My son-in-law as he was at the time was there. He said 'I'll do it,' and so he did. That was the end of my coaching career.

I failed at coaching Richard's cricket team because I wasn't competent to do it. I didn't know enough about cricket to coach the game, which is no surprise. As you know, I hated bloody cricket.

When he got a bit older, Richard worried me with his driving. He was a good young bloke—until he climbed behind the wheel of a car. He started off with a little Torana, then traded up to a big Torana, one of the V8s. One time when he was seventeen he was coming down the road from Black Mountain. It's your typical mountain road, windy and steep. The V8 Torana had a foot handbrake, which I absolutely hate in a motor car. I never found out if it was Richard or one of his mates, but someone put their foot on the brake and next thing they're coming tail-first down the road. I hope that put the wind up him, because it certainly put the wind up me once I found out.

After the Torana Richard moved on to a shagging wagon, one of those sinbin panel vans all lined with velvet inside. It looked real comfy. Every time he went out in it the coppers would pull him up. He had to get rid of it in the end because the coppers wouldn't leave him alone. Even if they didn't book him they'd pull him over and pester him.

Richard's taste in cars hasn't changed much over the years. He recently bought a $100,000 V8 Commodore with four pipes out the back and a bloody big motor that burns $30 of petrol just to make some noise!

Richard turned out to be an excellent carpenter and builder. When he was in high school he made a chess table and a little step ladder for us. They required the kind of detailed joinery that many carpenters never learn. I spent a lot of time with him on building sites when he was learning his trade. Compared with his sisters I gave Richard extra attention, that's true.

Diane takes after me in more ways than one. We both cry at the drop of a hat. Not that I'm a blubber-guts but if I encounter something happy or something sad, I just get emotional. Diane's more academic than Del. I'm no academic, but if I'd gone on with school I would have been. Mind you, I refused to go on with school, so it's no one's fault but mine!

Christine takes after Del. Del was into hockey and tennis, and Christine loves her sport. She enjoys the tennis,

Del on Copper who only had 3 good legs so easy for the kids to learn on.

Me on Light Star. A really enjoyable horse to ride.

Family phot taken at Christine's wedding to Christopher Beinke.

and travels down to Melbourne for the Australian Open. I played cricket and rugby league but I wasn't any good at either of them. I just made up the numbers. I was all right at Rugby League, I was a front row forward, but any goose can do that.

Because I was a keen horseman, I bought some horses to keep up at a farm. Christine and Richard loved them. Christine went in the show and got some points for her riding. Diane wasn't interested—she was more academic.

Family photo taken on our 40th wedding anniversary.

Christine has a lot of fine qualities. She's very supportive of Del and me, and gives us a lot of her time. She takes us for drives on Sunday for lunch or afternoon tea—she doesn't have to, I know she has other things to do.

Richard and I are very different. He definitely takes after Del—he's calmer than I am. Christine is very fiery—in that way she's like me. I'm usually calm but if I feel someone is putting it over me, I really get the shits. Richard is like Del—very calm and easy going.

Grandchildren

Del looked after the grandchildren a lot when they were little. She worked in the Commonwealth Government Printing Office here for eighteen years. Christine had a part-time job, and Del would knock off work at 1.00 PM so she could look after Christine's three children. Same thing with Jenny, Richard's former partner. Jenny had postnatal depression and wasn't coping, so Del would go over to their place and help Jenny with the cleaning.

We used to take food out to Richard and Jenny. Richard went through a bit of a rough patch himself, so we did what we could to help them out. During this time, he built himself a house. That project gave him something to focus on, and as you would expect, he did an excellent job as a carpenter.

For me, I couldn't really understand what he was going through, so I didn't handle it well. I didn't talk to him about it. Del had a motherly understanding—probably because she had her own experience with her thyroid problems.

Grandkids are funny creatures. One thing I've noticed over the years is that Christine's three children seem a little more attentive to us than Richard's four. Don't get me wrong—all seven of them will help you out if you ask them, but with Christine's three there's just that extra feeling of closeness. I've given this a lot of thought, because I've seen the same thing play out in my family when I was young.

Usually—not always—the daughter will bring her children back to her mother's side. So if you have a son who marries, his children are more likely to have that close connection with their maternal grandmother. Sometimes, of course, a son may stay close to his father, or maybe one set of grandparents, or maybe the children will be close to all their grandparents. I'm just saying what I've noticed. When I was growing up we were friends with our cousins on Dad's side of the family, but we had more to do with Mum's brothers' and sisters' kids. They all gravitated to that side of the family.

Now I'm not saying there's a whole lot of science in this. It's just my observations. After all, mothers and daughters are the heart of every family. But all our grandchildren matter to Del and me. They and their parents have their own lives to live, so it's good to see them whenever you can. Whenever we have a special event, like out 60th wedding anniversary or my 80th birthday, they turn up in droves. They're all extremely well-spoken, and while we'd like to see more of them, we realise they have to do their own thing.

We have seven grandkids. Three of them we see more than the other four, but if you rang them they'd be around in a flash. They're friendly, and they share things with us over the computer, but they don't often call around.

Richard has four boys. Two of them have red hair—a deep auburn colour. Matthew the youngest one takes after his father, a very good soccer player represented ACT. Very good with his hands he is proving to be a terrific carpenter.

Trevor the eldest is taller than me. I'm nominally six foot

The grandchildren. Matthew, Trevor, Katie, Alice, Jake, Thomas & Daniel.

Trevor, Seth (great grandchild), me & Del.

and he's three or four inches taller than me. He is a good style of bloke.

Then there's, Jake. Jake studied dancing. He's an absolutely beautiful fantastic dancer. He and his girlfriend Jacinda got

Jake & great grandchild Ned.

married in March 2017. Their new baby is a fine young lad called Ned and to everyone's delight he is a redhead.

Finally there is Daniel, terrific at all sports as well, and a very good gymnast. Took up the trade of hairdressing and is doing very well.

My father was the only boy in his family, and I was the only boy in mine. I had one boy and two girls. Richard wanted a girl, but he has four boys. Funny how these things turn out.

We have a great grandchild called Seth, who we don't see. He's a beautiful little fellow and we had a bit to do with him until he was three. Then Trevor, split with his partner. It didn't end well, and as a result we don't see him anymore. You know, the usual story.

Seth would be about seven now, a gorgeous looking little kid with blonde hair. He takes after Del's side. Del is blonde, with the tiniest bit of grey coming through now. She never dyed it. Over the years it got darker, but she'd get her highlights done. She'd have bits of foil in her hair sticking up like crests on the water. She stopped doing that twenty years ago. I'm just jealous. I wish I had some hair so I could get my tips done!

Mum and George

After I inherited the farm, I still had Mum to look after. Dad had died, so Mum was my responsibility. Del talked me into selling the farm and using the proceeds to buy a unit for Mum in Sydney, which I did.

We found her a nice two-bedroom unit in Kingsford, with a pleasant outlook. The unit had balconies, which was unusual for Sydney at the time. By this time, she had met George, the ex-jockey. I couldn't stand him. I thought he was a creep. George and Mum married as soon as we bought the unit. It was obvious that he wanted his slice of the cake. He thought it was his place.

1975 my Mum's birthday. Joan, Pauline, me, Pat & Mum.

As Mum became older and feebler, my sister Joan talked me into selling the Sydney unit and buying a new unit in Goulburn. Joan was working as a nurse there, so she could help look after Mum. So we sold the unit for $145,000 and then the Olympics came to Sydney and the price of real estate tripled. If we'd hung on to the unit it would have easily been worth $400,000. But that never worried me. Easy come, easy go.

My Mum's 80th birthday

Once Mum got to Goulburn she never stopped whingeing about the place and blaming me for it. I remember visiting her one time after Del and I had been down the coast. We'd had a fantastic holiday, relaxing for two weeks, but as soon as we visited my mother she let me have it. She started complaining about the place we bought for her. We'd set it up with her with everything new: television, washing machine, fridge and furniture. We spent several thousand dollars to make sure it was set up nicely for her.

She was carrying on about the kids over the road. When she sat by the window in the sun those kids must have thought she was looking at them, so they'd poke their tongues out at her. Apparently this was all my fault. She was upset and started blaming me.

I let her have it. I said, 'I'm not putting up with this shit every time I come here. I've been on holidays, I've had a great time, and when I come here it's all spoiled. Can you pick on someone else? It wasn't me that got you here. It was Joan, and she wanted you to move because she lives in Goulburn. And she's done a great job looking after you.'

Mum got the shock of her life when I went off at her. She never picked on me again. I couldn't have done it earlier because I idolised her. I had her up on a pedestal, which is pretty much how I treat Del. I'm the Duke and Del's the Queen.

The way Mum treated me, she must have thought I was a dickhead. But my sisters told me she only said positive things about me. I couldn't see it because she attacked me for the smallest things.

When Mum died George thought the unit passed onto him. His niece certainly thought he owned it—he lived there and he'd been telling everyone it was his. Silly old bastard.

So George got a big shock. As did his family, particularly his niece who was acting on his behalf when she rang me up. I'd asked a solicitor to draw up a contract for him to lease the unit. I knew the solicitor pretty well because I'd done work for him. He asked me if I thought I was being a little harsh. 'No,' I said, 'it's not harsh, I need it in writing with these people because the proverbial's going to hit the fan.'

George didn't like the terms of the lease so I pissed him off. Del and I sold the unit and put the money into an allocated pension. George went up to Queensland and bought an on-site mobile home next to one of his sons. None of his family seemed to have much money. Not that I feel any responsibility for him. He enjoyed a rails run all those years he lived with my mother.

Retirement

By 2000, when I was sixty-five and tired by the demanding physical work of building I decided to retire. Actually, I have to thank Diane for that. We were visiting her in Sydney. She said, 'You look terrible.'

I said, 'I'm absolutely knackered. I'm tired of working so hard.'

She said, 'Then don't do it.'

I said, 'I can't afford to stop work.'

She said, 'Of course you can. You've got a bit of money

Del & me on my 70th birthday.

saved, and you can get the part pension.' She talked me around.

I'd never really looked into it before. I came home, gave my work away, and knocked off. I found that difficult, at first. I thought I would go mad. I thought, 'Hell's bells, little bloody tadpoles, what am I going to do now?'

After a break at the beach, I returned in a better frame of mind and relaxed into retirement, only to discover that the phone started ringing with people asking for me to do small carpentry jobs for them. No concreting or bricklaying, and not so much climbing on roofs. Roof trusses are mostly prefabricated now, but there were still occasions when I was asked to cut a roof in. So, I resumed work at a much more leisurely pace for another ten years. I relished working on my own at my own pace and without responsibility for employees.

Me & Del enjoying a coffee.

I am now fully retired and spend time with my beautiful wife of sixty years, Del, my sisters Pat and Pauline and their families, and my wonderful children, grandchildren and friends.

Me & Del celebrating our 60th wedding anniversary at Old Parliament House.

Waiting to celebrate our
60th wedding anniversary
at Old Parliament House

Me at 80.

Del at 80.

Me & Del enjoying Jake's wedding.

Brian Dromgold

A very happy Frogmore Farmer.

CHAPTER EIGHTEEN

Brian's reflections on a life well-lived
A nice bloke?

When you reach the grand age of eighty you're entitled to sit back and reflect on a life well-lived. From the outset I tried to be the opposite of my dad. I wasn't aware of this. It wasn't a conscious decision. But I didn't agree with his drinking. So I guess subconsciously I set out to do the opposite.

At the same time, he had some positive qualities. He was basically a nice bloke, it's just the grog got him. I took the good bits—his ability to work hard—and avoided the worst of him.

Am I a nice bloke? I was discussing this with a woman who came to do some cleaning for us a while back. We were talking about people she has trouble getting on with. I said, with some trepidation I might add, 'How would you describe me, Amy?'

She said, 'I'd say you're one of the nicest blokes to get along with I've ever met.' So there you go! Other people think I'm a decent person. I don't do anyone any harm. Not purposely anyway. But how decent am I? It's really up to others to judge.

I just see myself as an everyday bloke without too many bad habits. Mind you, if you saw our garbage bin at the moment you might think differently. It's stuffed full of garbage with old shoes and bits of hose sticking out the top. But the bloke over the road with one leg—it's him what done it! He cleaned half the stuff out of my garage the other day and put it in the bin. I wouldn't overfill it like that. He said, 'No it's fine—it'll be alright.' He's going on holidays and I'm putting his bin out tonight, so I might go and put the overflow in his bin.

Is that what you'd call a nice bloke? I guess it depends on whether or not you get caught.

Is there anything I dislike about myself? Not really, unless you're talking about growing old. I don't like the fact that I've lost my hair. I used to have a decent head of hair, but now it's disappearing. And I don't like getting these cancers being cut out of my skin. That's the price I have to pay, working in the sun all those years. But those are just symptoms of age. Apart from that, I'm pretty much content.

Steptoe and Son

Del doesn't read. I do. I love my books. Westerns, mostly. On TV I love English comedy, and mostly watch the ABC because it has English comedy, Australian content, and no ads. Del likes *My Kitchen Rules*, but I can't stand those kinds of shows. To me, they're phoney. Modern comedy can be a little sad. I prefer older shows like *Steptoe and Son*. They call me Steptoe sometimes for the rubbish I keep in my garage. But I'm not that bad.

Every New Year people ask me if I'm going to clear out the garage. No, no, no and no! I don't see it as a problem. Del and I have a good understanding—I keep what I have in the garage. It's my domain. My man cave.

What's in there? Mostly old stuff I never use. When I'm dead, the kids will throw it on the tip. I've got rabbit traps, horse collars, an old-fashioned horse drench, wire strainers, a milk separator—not a big one, but one we used on the farm. It's mostly old farming gear. I don't see it as vintage memorabilia. I don't believe it's worth money, either, and there's a good reason for this.

I've got an old wash stand with a marble top and a tiled area on the back. It's maybe three feet or so foot across, with rails on either side for hanging your towels. We used it to clean our boots at the farm—that's how old it was. When I brought it over from the farm it was all smashed up, so in my wisdom I decided to fix it. The bottom piece was missing, so I remade it out of Australian red cedar. The uprights that held the towel rails were originally made from turned pieces of timber. I didn't have a lathe so I put a ring around the timber and held it against the edge of a grinder. They turned out looking really good.

Once it was done I took it to the dealers to see what it was worth. I thought four hundred dollars, maybe five hundred. I get there and the bloke says, 'You shouldn't have bloody touched it, mate. You've stuffed it up. Leave these things as they are.' He looked down his nose at me. 'I could give you one hundred,' he said.

I went away with my tail between my legs. When I came home I put it back in the garage. I was absolutely disgusted, because I'd gone to a lot of trouble, and that bastard treated me like a fool.

So there might be a lot of stuff hanging there, but no one values it. There's an old breast drill with a gear system. You put the curved part against your chest and leaned on it hard, held the side bit with your left hand and turned the other side with your right hand—you could put a lot of pressure into it. There's also an old-fashioned brace and bit with no ratchet. You just put the bit in. We drilled all the fence posts with it. We had nothing electrical or motorised on our farm. Never even had a tractor. We lived the life of those people in America—the Amish. Apart from the motorbikes and cars—we never drove a buggy to church. But if it meant putting your back into your work—no doubt in the world about it.

Flying

Anytime I've had to fly I've forced myself to go. I've flown to Sydney twice and Brisbane twice. That's about it. It was bloody awful being in the plane. The first time I flew to Sydney my brother-in-law suggested having a couple of whiskeys beforehand. I was travelling to Sydney for my Mum's birthday party, and the whiskey helped numb my brain. I can't remember if I had a whiskey on the way back because I was absolutely petrified.

I also travelled to Sydney twice when Del was crook. She was taken by air ambulance, and my daughter drove me down to Sydney. I stayed in a motel next to the hospital, and then Del and I flew back to Canberra together.

On one of our trips to Brisbane Diane had upgraded us to business class without telling us. I said to Del, 'This is fantastic!' but I didn't like how the whole plane was creaking and groaning as if it was going to fall apart when we landed.

On the way back from Brisbane we didn't have the advantage of an upgrade, and ended up seated down the back next to the toilet, with the arse of the plane dragging on the tarmac. So that turned me off flying again—although it's really Uncle John I have to thank!

Drinking and smoking

For what it's worth, here's my philosophy on drinking. Never drink so much that you lose control of your faculties, your wits or your bowels. If someone wants to take you on you need to be in control. Alcohol definitely slows your reflexes.

I'm not in favour of drugs. When I was fourteen I was hooked on cough medication briefly, but that's all. I smoked for many years but never heavily. I never felt I had to have a cigarette, unless I got frustrated on the job. Then I'd come home, sit on the pavers under the pergola, and have a stubby and cigarette. Honest truth? I absolutely enjoyed it.

I've got five pipes here in a bowl: two curly ones and three straight ones. Just the other day I said to Del, 'I might buy a packet of tobacco and stoke one of them pipes up.'

She said 'That's fine, you can smoke it in the garage.'

Two of our kids still smoke—Christine and Richard. I'll say to the grandkids, 'Don't smoke in front of us.' They still smoke, you can smell it on them. Whenever Richard goes out for a smoke I'll go and stand with him and smell the smoke wafting across.

Richard smokes tailor-mades. They never smell as good as rollies. Rollies stick to your bottom lip and keep going out, but what can you do? I just love the smell.

Travel

I've never travelled outside Australia, although I have been to Queensland. That's different enough. Del and I were planning a holiday in Fiji, but I broke my leg—Del says on purpose. I still have my passport, so who knows?

I've never had an urge to travel to Ireland, despite my

heritage. When I think of Ireland I think of the slums, the poverty, whole families dying in the Potato Famine. Then you had the Catholics and Protestants killing each other. Just terrible. One thing I would like to see is one of those little Irish pubs in the centre of town. Where violinists play those old Irish folk songs and everyone else is singing along or dancing close. When I imagine this I hear Daniel O'Donnell, the Irish country singer, crooning along inside my head.

The pergola problem

I've got a problem at the moment that's eating at me. There's a pergola at the back of the house. It has a pitched roof covered with shadecloth, and it's a decent size, maybe eight metres by three and a half. It's got dry rot in it. I've had dry rot in it several times over the years. I built it out of Oregon originally, it's the worst stuff I ever came across. I kept replacing a rafter here, a rafter there. I've replaced so many it's a wonder it hasn't fallen down. You can hardly see where I've repaired it but now it needs a major facelift.

I've gone over to treated pine now. Fair dinkum, you wouldn't feed Oregon to the cattle. I used to think it was great stuff, but it still must be half green when it comes out of America. We were hoodwinked by it. They've banned it in building in Canberra, and in NSW too. They won't actually let them use it.

So I need to replace the main beam. I know exactly what to do. Prop everything up, cut the beams out—I could do it standing on my head if I had someone to do the high bits. I've spoken with Richard about it, but we've never hammered out all the details. This is the problem being a retired builder, and getting older. You know what to do, you've proven yourself over and over again, but now it's just beyond you. It's very frustrating. My back's gone, my pergola's falling down, and I need some help.

Religion

When you die you go into the ground, that's where you go. No pearly gates. Maybe there's a hell. Churches exist to keep the money rolling in. Don't get me wrong. I'm a believer; I just don't know what I believe in. I was brought up a strict Catholic and Del was brought up as a strict Methodist, and we both believe basically the same thing. What do we believe? That it's all a big mystery. When people have nothing precise to turn to they all believe in something a bit different.

I was in church recently for a funeral, in a big cathedral. When I enter a place like that first thing I do is look up. Not to see if God's there, but to make sure nothing falls on me! Make sure none of those bloody great beams are going to come down on my head. That's the builder and fireman in me.

When they all go up for holy communion I feel a bit of a twang in my stomach. It's just a glass of wine and a little wafer. All the good Catholics stream up to get their wafer. They put it in your hand now, not on your tongue like they used to. I'm thinking, 'Will I or won't I?' Then I tell myself, 'Don't be a hypocrite.' You never lose that sense that you should step up and take that wafer, it's been drilled into you so long and hard.

What disappoints me is the way they've treated those boys in their orphanages and the church. We looked up to the priests, and for what? It's horrific that so many priests had a taste for young boys. I saw through the church when I was twelve.

Success

What's my greatest success in life? There's no question: marrying Del and having three beautiful kids. Our kids cause us no real grief at all. They've all been beautiful kids. They've had some medical issues, which are curable, but they were still beautiful kids, never nasty to us or troublesome. Apart from Christine topping up the whiskey bottle with cold tea when she was twelve or thirteen. But we just laughed about it. We didn't jump up and down or carry on.

So family comes first with me. As far as my career goes, there were three significant achievements: getting into the police force, then the fire brigade, then getting my building licence in the ACT. I'd always wanted to be a policeman and a fireman. As far as building went, I never even thought I'd need a licence. Things just happened for me. I didn't even think or worry about them. There's been a sense of progression as I've gone through life. I've learned there's no such thing as an obstacle. Just problems waiting to be solved.

The secret to a happy marriage

Del and I were married on Easter Saturday in 1956 in the Crookwell Methodist Church, so we have recently celebrated our 60th wedding anniversary! At the celebration I got up to give a speech and I found it hard because my emotions welled up. Same as my 80th birthday party—when I saw Del sitting at the end of the table I couldn't go on. I just came over all teary. Christine came to my aid. She stood beside me and told everyone the things I wanted to say. I was emotional because Del had been so sick two-and-a-half years ago. It means so much to me, being with her for all these years.

We were pretty surprised and proud to get letters from the Queen and Governor General of Australia congratulating us on our 60th wedding anniversary. So the question on everyone's lips is the same: *how did you do it?*

Del will tell you we've never had an argument. I put this down to her, not me. She has more tolerance than me. Del believes you should never let the sun go down on an argument. So before you go to sleep, you talk things out. We talk a lot. We never have the radio on in the car, so we can talk about the things we see going past. We make up stories and just enjoy talking with each other.

If we do have a difference of opinion, we change the subject. It's better to talk about something different than having an argument you can't win.

From my point of view, we struggled a lot in the early days but we made it through by working together. We were just so pleased to be able to earn a living and survive. I was tired from working two jobs at once, which left me with no time to squabble or fight.

So I'd say the secret to a happy marriage is to work the husband half to death, and program him to say 'Yes, dear.' I don't think I've changed during all the time we've been married. After sixty years, I'm still saying 'Yes, dear'!

www.ingramcontent.com/pod-product-compliance
Lightning Source LLC
Chambersburg PA
CBHW040250170426
43191CB00018B/2365